TUCKER
SIGNING STRATEGIES
FOR READING

Tucker, Bethanie H., Ed.D.
    Tucker Signing Strategies for Reading
Bethanie H. Tucker © 2001. 162 pp.
    ISBN 1-929229-10-0

1. Reading   2. Education   3. Title

Also by Bethanie H. Tucker, Ed.D.

Mr. Base Ten Invents Mathematics

BETHANIE H. TUCKER

TUCKER
SIGNING STRATEGIES
FOR READING

aha!

Process, Inc.

ACKNOWLEDGMENTS

Special thanks to:

Dr. Jackie Hager, principal of Southside Elementary School, Pittsylvania County, Virginia, research partner.

Beth Dulaney and Michelle Dove, students at Averett College, Danville, Virginia, who first field-tested the Tucker Signing Strategies for Reading.

Anna Hamlett, my niece and hand-sign model for this book's photos.

Danville School District principals, teachers, and children.

William Tucker, my husband, who encouraged my research.

ABOUT THE AUTHOR

Dr. Bethanie H. Tucker of Alton, Virginia, created hand signs for a phonetic reading strategy out of a desire to help students of varying skill levels learn to read and enjoy the journey of reading. Her greatest pleasure is watching children who have struggled with reading discover that letters and sounds are not such a great mystery after all.

Dr. Tucker holds three academic degrees, all in education: a B.S. from Averett College, Danville, and an M.S. and Ed.D. from the University of Virginia, Charlottesville. She is associate professor of education at Averett College.

If you have questions about Tucker Signing Strategies for Reading, contact Dr. Tucker through our Website at www.ahaprocess.com or call our office at (800) 424-9484.

TABLE OF CONTENTS

Part I: Lessons   Part II: Student Pages

Lessons	Page	Text	Student Page
1 – long *e*	24	*eeeee*	116
2 – *m*	26	*Me*	117
3 – *s*	28	*See me.*	118
4 – *w*	30	*We see.*	119
5 – short *u*	32	*See us.*	120
6 – long *i*	34	*I see ...*	121
7 – *b*	36	*bees!*	122
8 – *n* (and silent *e*)	38	*Nine bees ...*	123
9 – *z*	40	*buzz.*	124

Lessons	**Page**	**Text**	**Student Page**
30 – *th*	82	*A thin sheep with thick hair came by. The thin sheep sat by the pig.*	145
31 – *ing*	84	*But the pig kept sleeping, so the sheep got up and kept going.*	146
32 – *x*	86	*Next a fox came by. "You need a bath," she said. The fox kept running, and the pig kept sleeping.*	147
33 – long *u*	88	*A cute mule trotted up to the pig. "Hi, pig. You are cute, but you need a bath," he said. Then the mule kept going, and the pig kept sleeping.*	148
34 – *y* (long *e*)	92	*A pony named Tony trotted up. "That pig smells funny," he said. Then the pony kept going, and the pig kept sleeping.*	149
35 – *ow/ou*	94	*A cow came by and said with a frown, "Wow. How did a pink pig get so brown? You need a bath now." Then the cow kept going, and the pig kept sleeping.*	150
36 – *wh*	96	*A white rabbit with whiskers came hopping by. "That is a messy pig," he said. "Why are you so dirty, and when did you play in the mud?" But the pig kept sleeping, so the white rabbit kept hopping.*	151
37 – *y* (consonant)	98	*A duck and her duckling came by. "Yuck," said the duck. Her duckling said, "Yes, that is a yucky pig." Then the ducks kept going, and the pig kept sleeping.*	152

Lessons	Page	Text	Student Page
38 – *ch*	100	*A bird hopped by. "Chirp, chirp. Such a messy chum," the bird sang. But the pig kept sleeping, so the bird kept hopping.*	153
39 – *ar*	102	*It got dark. The pig was still far from home.*	154
40 – long *oo*	104	*A goose flew by. "You are too dirty," said the goose. "The new moon will be out soon." Then the goose kept flying, and the pig kept sleeping.*	155
41 – *v*	106	*Five deer ran by. "You are very dirty," one deer said. "You should dive into the lake." The five deer kept running, while the pig kept sleeping.*	156
42 – short *oo*	108	*An owl took a look at the pig. She shook her wings. "Just look," she said. "Go jump into the brook." The owl did not stop. She just kept flying, and the pig kept sleeping.*	157
43 – *aw*	110	*Last of all a skunk named Paul crawled up to the pig. The pig woke up. She saw the skunk. "Hello," said the pig. The skunk was glad to have a friend. "You smell nice," said the skunk. "So do you," said the pig. The skunk said, "I will walk all the way home with you."*	158

INTRODUCTION

Phonics Instruction

Learning to read involves recognizing the printed symbols for words. Children learn to read printed text in a number of ways. Words instantly recognized are part of the child's sight vocabulary. The context in which a word is found can contribute to one's ability to recognize certain words, such as the word *stop* on a stop sign. Instruction in the acquisition of sight vocabulary and contextual-clue recognition is an essential component of any reading program.

A third vital component of reading instruction is phonetic analysis. In order to grasp the fundamentals of the reading process, children must learn that printed letters represent speech sounds. Phonics instruction involves teaching the relationship between printed letters and the speech sounds they represent.

Of the three interrelated reading skills – sight vocabulary, contextual clues, and phonetic analysis – the latter is frequently the most difficult for children to master, primarily because learning letter-sound relationships is totally different from the child's previous life experiences. Additional difficulties stem from the fact that letter shapes are arbitrary and abstract. There is no logical relationship between the appearance of the letter and the sound it represents – no inherent clues to assist the child in remembering the associated sound.

A child attempting to read a word containing the letter *p,* for example, obviously can see the printed letter on the page. His/her task is to remember the speech sound represented by the printed symbol and blend that speech sound with others that surround it. The goal of the signing strategy is to provide a tool to assist the reader in accomplishing this task.

Research Findings

The strategy of signing phonetic sounds has been field-tested with children and adults from a variety of backgrounds in various settings, including one-on-one and large-group instruction in public and private schools – and among home-schooled children and private tutorials. With certain modifications determined by the needs of the child, the program is effective with all populations and in any environment.

Research shows that the signing strategy has been successful in meeting the original goal of the program – to build a bridge between printed symbols and the speech sounds they represent. Children move almost immediately from learning the signs to using them to decode unfamiliar words. Children who have been taught this strategy frequently are observed moving their hands to decode words when reading for pleasure and when reading from Science and Social Studies texts during silent reading and oral recitations.

In addition to building a bridge between letters and speech sounds, several surprising (yet equally important) benefits have been identified.

1. **Because the signing inherent in the strategy interjects movement into the reading process, many very active students demonstrate the ability and the desire to read for longer blocks of time when using the hand signs.** The reading act naturally includes visual clues in the form of printed words; auditory clues are added when the teacher and the students pronounce the sounds that the printed letters represent. The process is typically devoid, however, of kinesthetic involvement. The Tucker hand signs not only allow for, but actually require, bodily involvement to become part of the reading process. This movement component particularly benefits the child whose preferred learning style is kinesthetic/tactile, which some studies indicate may be as many of 80% of young readers. Whatever the learning style, all children need to move about in order to release excess energy. Although slight, the movement included in hand signing allows for some energy release, enabling the learner to concentrate more intently and for longer periods of time.

2. **Benefits to boys and ADHD students are immediate and dramatic.** Perhaps because most boys are naturally active, and certainly because ADHD (attention-deficit hyperactivity disorder) children, the majority of whom are boys, are quite active, these groups of students have demonstrated the most immediate positive reaction to, and appear to have derived the greatest benefits from, the hand-signs. Teachers and parents of learning-disabled and mentally challenged children also have reported success with the strategy.

3. **Requiring children to attempt an unfamiliar word using hand signs shifts the onus of responsibility for solving a word from the teacher to the child.** When confronted with an unfamiliar word, beginning readers sometimes stare at an object or look intently at their teachers, waiting for help. By reminding the child to sign the word the teacher is saying, "You have the power to read this word." Children no longer need to wait for someone to do the work for them. This sense of self-empowerment transfers very quickly to new reading situations. The signing strategy identifies tools – the hands – that almost always are readily available to the child.

4. **A surprising result of the *Tucker Signing Strategies for Reading* has been the degree to which children enjoy using the hand signs.** Many appear to view this experience as learning a special sign language (or even "secret code"), with learning to read an added bonus. They come to enjoy identifying the "special" signs and chunks in words. As a result, they learn to look at the entire word rather than guessing the word based on the initial consonant or syllable. The program also makes learning some phonetic rules less of a burden because the children enjoy making the associated signs.

5. **The signing strategy cues teachers to the students' thought processes.** Children typically reveal very few clues as to what they are thinking as they gaze at

an unfamiliar word. The overt behaviors involved in the signing process provide insight for the teacher as to what mental processes are taking place in the child's mind. The requirement to sign is in essence a requirement to think out loud.

6. **Learning the hand signs requires little effort for most children.** The author's initial concern over "adding to the curriculum" proved to be unfounded. Most children of first-grade age or older learn all 44 signs in two or three half-hour sessions. Younger children naturally need to learn the signs and the associated speech sounds at a slower, more developmentally appropriate pace.

7. **Adults report that they benefit from learning the signs.** A number of adults have been taught to read using the Tucker signing strategies. They report that when in an environment where they don't want to use the signs, they can think about them and thereby remember the associated speech sounds.

TUCKER SIGNING STRATEGIES FOR READING

Tucker Signing Strategies for Reading is designed to prompt associations between letters and the sounds they represent. The prompts are hand signs. The program includes a hand sign for each letter and some letter combinations that represent distinct speech sounds. The Tucker hand signs are different from the signs of American Sign Language. Each hand sign is designed to resemble, to the greatest extent possible, the shape and the sound of the letter it represents. The hand sign for the letter *p,* for example, is shaped like the letter *p* and is held in front of the lips as the *p* sound is pronounced. The sign, therefore, builds a bridge between the printed letter and the associated speech sound.

Guidelines for Teaching Reading Using Hand Signs

1. **All hand signs must be made with the left hand.** Many letter shapes appear backwards when signed with the right hand (see LESSON 1: long *e*). Naturally, some children (and many adults) who are right-handed initially resist using the left hand. Research in the Tucker signing strategies demonstrates that …

   A. Signing with the left hand is not difficult. Right-handed children demonstrate very little if any frustration forming the signs with their left hand. While a few children need to be reminded regularly at first to use their left hand, a quick and casual verbal prompt usually suffices.

   B. After some practice, resistance to left-handed signing quickly diminishes or disappears. Children can be encouraged to use their left hand in a number of ways. Some teachers instruct the children to hold an object in their right hand while signing, which makes it impossible for them to sign with the incorrect hand. Another successful strategy is to provide the children with yarn bracelets that slip easily over their hands – and to which small bells have been tied. The bracelets can be slipped over the right hand, with the warning that no bells should be heard – or over the left hand, with the invitation to "let the signs ring."

   C. After the initial presentation of each sign, the child rarely <u>looks</u> at the shape of his/her hand when signing; therefore, the kinesthetic involvement becomes more important than the visual appearance of the letter in sparking the appropriate letter-sound relationship. Thus many teachers choose not to correct children who occasionally forget to use the left hand at this point but are experiencing success decoding words.

2. **Students <u>must</u> make the letter speech/sound(s) as they make each sign.** This simultaneous "signing," "seeing," and "saying" strengthens letter shape/sound associations and creates a multi-modal learning situation.

3. **New signs should be demonstrated in isolation very briefly, then immediately blended with other letters in the context of a word.** When a word is signed, the individual letter signs should be blended into one continuous motion, flowing smoothly from one letter into the next. When signing the word *no,* for example, the *n* sign and *n* sound should be made distinctly, stretching the *n* sound. Then, without breaking the sounds of the word, the left hand should move downward into the *o* sign as the *n* sound blends into the *o* sound, completing the word *no.* Beginning with LESSON 2, each new sound is presented in the context of a word. Each new word and all other words in the children's story pages in the second half of the manual contain the new letter combined with previously taught letters only, so the child should be able to read each page in the story independently, with the help of the hand signs.

4. **Blends and other common letter combinations should be signed as one unit – or chunk.** These blends – or chunks – should be practiced as a unit whenever they are encountered. When teaching the word *horse,* for example, the teacher would point out the *or* chunk, and students would practice signing *or* several times. The teacher also would prompt students to recognize the silent *e* at the end of the word. The word would then be signed *h-or-s* (silent *e*). Students should later be prompted to recognize the *or* chunk in additional words. Other word chunks to point out and practice include *oy, oi,* and consonant blends. When teaching the word *brisk,* for example, the *br* blend should be recognized and practiced, then the *sk* blend addressed. The reason the letter *i* represents the short-*i* sound should subsequently be discussed. Finally, the word *brisk* would be signed *br-i-sk.* Tucker hand signs have been formulated for certain very distinctive word chunks, such as *tion, sh, ch, ow, ou,* and *r*-controlled vowels.

5. **Students should <u>discontinue</u> use of the hand signs when they are reading immediately recognizable words.** The researcher was initially concerned about students relying too heavily on the hand signs, allowing them to become permanent crutches. This concern also was unfounded. Children automatically drop the hand signs upon recognition of a word or words. On many occasions a child will need to sign only one word in a sentence – or perhaps only a portion of a word. If, for example, a student can read the *see* portion of the word *seeing,* he/she should be encouraged to read *see,* sign *ing,* then put the word parts together and solve the word.

6. **Rules of phonetic analysis must be taught.** The Tucker hand signs assist children in recalling letter-sound relationships and blending sounds to make words. They do not, however, hold any secrets for teaching phonetic rules, other than the fact that the hand signs sometimes make learning rules more fun. Research demonstrates, for example, that many children enjoy decoding words that end with silent *e* using the signing strategy because they enjoy making the silent-*e* sign. Many children also enjoy looking for special signable chunks in a word before they attempt to read it. This level of enjoyment can occur only after rules have been taught through both the signing strategy <u>and</u> those strategies that teachers typically employ.

7. **Long-vowel sounds are presented before short vowels.** Because long-vowel sounds "say" the vowel names and therefore are easier for children to remember, they are presented before short vowels in this manual. Signs for long-vowel sounds are basically the same as short-vowel signs. Long-vowel signs *a, e,* and *o* are made at waist level; the short-vowel signs are made with the hand held higher in the air. Similar modifications apply to *i, y,* and *u.* More detailed explanations are provided in the lessons in which these letters are presented.

8. **Irregularly spelled words can be handled a number of ways.**

   A. Words that are frequently encountered and do not follow regular spelling rules should be presented as sight vocabulary, with a brief explanation that they break the rules of phonetics and, therefore, cannot be signed.

   Examples of **SIGHT VOCABULARY WORDS** include:

does	done	friends	give	have
here	know	love	many	more
none	of	once	one	put
said	should	snow	some	to
two	use	who	you	your

   B. When only a portion of the word contains an irregular spelling pattern, this "tricky part" can be pointed out and pronounced for the child, and the remainder of the word can be signed. An example would be the word *naughty.* It could be pointed out that the *gh* in this word is silent. Then the remainder of the word can be signed *n-au-t* and *y* (*e* sound).

   C. Families of words that contain irregular spelling patterns, such as *igh,* can be taught in one lesson. When presenting the word *light,* for example, the teacher would explain that the *gh* combination is silent, and the *i* sign will be made when *igh* is encountered. The word would then be signed with the *L,* long-*i, and t* signs. Additional words that belong to this word family should then be presented.

   D. Minimal-contrast sounds, such as the *zh* sound in *pleasure* and the distinction between the voiced and unvoiced *th* sound, should be acknowledged with little elaboration at this point. When teaching the word *pleasure,* for example, the teacher could simply say, "That *s* sounds a little like a *z,* doesn't it?" Children tend to accept these irregularities readily.

Manual Format

Part I of this manual is divided into 44 lessons, with one new hand sign introduced in each lesson. The lessons are sequenced for the emergent reader but can be rearranged or accelerated for more advanced readers.

Each lesson includes:

1. <u>A description and illustration of the new hand sign</u>.

2. <u>Procedures for teaching the lesson</u>.

3. <u>Extension and enrichment activities</u>. These activities suggest strategies for reinforcing each new letter sign. Although most activities are listed only once, many can be repeated for a number of letter signs. For example, the PICTURE DICTIONARY described in LESSON 2 could be continued for each new letter. Such activities as WATER WRITING described in LESSON 3 and SLOW RACE in LESSON 9 also can be repeated frequently. WORD CHALLENGE words, which are listed for most lessons, combine each new sign with previously taught letters to form new words, in addition to those found in the story.

4. <u>Student Take-Home Book Title</u>. Each lesson references a Student Take-Home Book with controlled vocabulary. These books are available through **aha!** Process, Inc. in a reproducible workbook format for students to read and take home.

Part II includes story pages that feature each lesson's focus word(s) in the context of previously taught words and letters. Each student page, which is to be illustrated by the student, contributes to an ongoing story. Student pages should be hole-punched and added to each child's individual storybook as they are completed.

BEGINNING THE PROGRAM

Emergent Readers

When working with children ages 5 and younger who are ready to learn to read, many teachers cover the first five or six lessons quickly, perhaps in one session. On Day 2 the previously taught letters can be reviewed and one or two new ones added. This approach sustains interest and allows students to feel an immediate sense of accomplishment, having learned to read several words in a short period of time.

More Advanced/Older Readers

More mature readers may not need to complete each lesson in its entirety and certainly will not need to complete every <u>extension</u> and <u>enrichment</u> activity suggested in the manual. More advanced readers would be expected to move quickly through individual letter signs, progressing immediately to blends, diphthongs, digraphs, affixes, and other word chunks. It is often more appealing to older readers to begin with the blends as opposed to the simpler signs, so that they can immediately read longer and more challenging words.

More advanced readers enjoy quickly learning the signs and using them to attack longer, more sophisticated words that follow regular spelling patterns. These words can be approached in a fashion similar to the way a detective would look for clues to solve a case. When attempting to solve these words, the reader should first identify such clues as blends, affixes, digraphs, diphthongs, *r*-controlled vowels, and other word chunks. The word *church,* for example, contains three word chunks: *ch, ur,* and *ch*, which the child could identify, sign, blend, and pronounce.

The list of regularly spelled words that appeal to children beyond the kindergarten level is virtually endless. Following is an introductory list:

aardvark	abash	abbreviation	abdomen	abduct
abduction	abide	ablaze	abound	abrupt
absorb	absorption	absurd	acceleration	accommodation
account	accumulation	action	activate	adder
addiction	addition	administration	admiration	admirer
admonition	adoption	adoration	adore	adorn
adverb	adverse	advertise	affection	affliction
afterburner	aftermath	afterward	aggravation	aground
ajar	alarm	alert	alive	allegation

allergic	alligator	allow	aloud	alternation
alternator	arch	auburn	auction	audit
auditory	augur	august	author	automatic
aviation	awkward	awning	battery	baud
bawl	bluster	bookkeeper	bracket	bravery
broker	caption	carbon	carp	carpenter
catcher	category	caucus	cauliflower	causation
cause	caustic	caution	chamber	chapter
char	chart	charter	cheddar	chew
chide	chirp	church	churn	coach
condition	confer	confine	confirm	convene
cower	crawl	cub	cube	cucumber
cutlery	cyclone	dawn	dermis	dervish
description	dinner	discord	dock	docket
edit	elevator	emotion	endive	erode
erupt	eruption	ether	ethic	expectation
expert	faucet	Faulkner	fault	fauna
fawn	femur	fender	fever	finite
flirt	flitter	flower	foundation	fraction
further	garland	gauze	gawk	govern
grant	grip	gripe	grist	hack
haul	haunt	hawk	hawker	Hawthorne
hermit	hinder	housekeeping	hyper	impart
incurs	induction	intercept	jaunt	jawbone
jury	landmark	landslide	larder	larva
laud	launch	launcher	laundry	laurel
lawful	lawless	lawyer	lease	liberty
lifelike	lobster	location	locomotion	lodestone
lotion	loud	makeshift	maul	medicate
mineral	motivation	muffler	nation	nausea
nautical	observation	option	orderly	otter
ouch	ounce	outbound	outburst	outcurve
outer	outgoing	outlaw	outline	outrun
outskirts	outstanding	outstation	outward	overcast
overhand	owl	parch	partner	partnership
Pauline	pauper	pause	pawn	penetrate
penicillin	peninsula	percolate	phase	poncho
pouch	pounce	poverty	power	prevent
proceed	profile	propose	prosper	Quaker
quarter	quartile	question	quiver	quota
quote	raw	recede	refer	release
resolute	return	rout	rubbish	rudder
sanction	saucer	sauna	sausage	saw
sawhorse	sawyer	scalp	scorch	score
scowl	scratch	sector	sharpen	shatter
sheepskin	shelve	shimmer	shirt	shower

shun	sling	sober	soccer	squawk
squelch	squint	squirm	squirt	stampede
starvation	substance	substitute	sunshine	taunt
tawny	temper	thermos	thorn	tilt
timber	tower	trickery	turnover	urchin
vacation	valve	vanish	vapor	vault
vaulted	violent	viper	vitamin	vivid
vocation	voice	volunteer	voucher	warn
warning	warp	wart	waste	waver
whiff	whimper	whirl	whiskers	whisper
wince	wintergreen	Yale	yam	yammer
yard	yarn	yawl	yawn	yestermorning
yippee	yodel	yoke	yolk	yucca
Yukon	zenith	zero	zigzag	zing
ZIP code	zipper	zippy	zone	zoom

When irregularly spelled words are presented to readers of all ages, the "tricky parts" (letters or letter combinations that do not follow regular pronunciation rules) should be pointed out before the child attempts the word.

Phonetic Organizer

Some children benefit from a phonetic organizer, such as a chart that lists the most frequent spellings of each vowel sound. The example below shows how a chart might look in its initial states; additional spellings and examples should be added to the chart as they are encountered.

a		e				i	
a (e)	cake	e	me	ey	key	i (e)	kite
ay	day	ee	see	ie	chief	y	my
ey	they	ea	meat	y	pony	igh	sight

o		u			
o	no	u (e)	cute		
o (e)	bone	ue	glue		
ow	show	ew	flew		
oa	boat				

In each case, the represented sound is signed. For example, when signing the word *say,* the *ay* would be signed with the long-*a* sign. The word *light* would be signed *L,* long *i, t*

TUCKER
SIGNING STRATEGIES
FOR READING

Lessons 1 - 44

LESSON 1 – long e

Note: *All letters should be signed with the left hand. If signed with the right hand, many letters, including the letter* e, *would face in the wrong direction.*

Sign Description

Curl the fingers of your left hand to resemble the shape of the letter *e*, as illustrated. Then extend your hand outward while making the long-*e* sound.

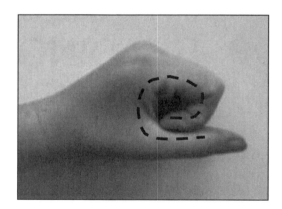 

(always use left hand)

Procedures

1. When demonstrating the long-*e* sign, the teacher should draw the letter *e* on his/her left hand with a washable marker.

2. Instruct students to look at the sign and make the *e* sound as they sign the letter. (Making the sound is a vital part of each sign and should be repeated for every letter.)

Student Page – #1

TEXT: eeeee

ILLUSTRATION: Draw a picture of yourself and something that frightens you and makes you say "eeeee."

Extension Activity

GIVE ME A SIGN: As the teacher reads a list of words, the students make the *e* sign (and sound) when they hear a word that contains the long-*e* sound. Sample words containing the long-*e* sound include *bead, bean, bee, breeze, believe, clean, dream, feed, he, me, mean, neat, need, season, see, seed, seen, she, and we.*

Enrichment Activity

HAND PAINTING: Instruct students to <u>paint</u> the letter *e* on their left hand using safe products, such as finger paint, chalk, pudding, etc.

Student Take-Home Book – *eeeee*

NOTES

LESSON 2 – *m*

Previously taught letter: long *e*

Lesson focus word: *Me*

Sign Description

Extend the three middle fingers of your left hand downward to resemble the letter *m,* as illustrated in Step 1. Place the tips of your extended fingers to your lips while making the *m* sound.

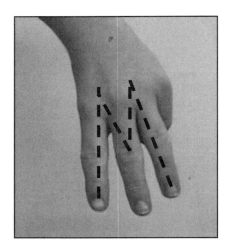

Procedures

1. Trace the *m* shape on your hand with a washable marker.

2. Demonstrate the *m* sign; instruct students to make the *m* sound as they sign the letter.

3. Review the *e* sign.

4. Demonstrate signing the letter *m*, stretching the *m* sound and flowing smoothly into the *e* sign and sound to form the word *me*. There should not be a break between the *m* sound and the *e* sound.

Student Page – #2

TEXT: Me

ILLUSTRATION: Draw a picture of yourself.

Extension Activities

FOOD CHAIN: Read a list of foods. Students respond to their favorites by making the *m* sign and *m* sound.

PICTURE DICTIONARY: Students will find magazine pictures of objects that begin with the letter *m* and glue the pictures to a page labeled *m.* Repeat this activity for subsequent lessons and combine pages to make PICTURE DICTIONARIES.

Enrichment Activity

SLOW SIGNS: Instruct the students to slowly sign the word *me* as one child writes it on the board. Repeat as additional children do the writing.

Student Take-Home Book – *Me?*

NOTES

for silient e make e with left hand cover it up with right hand

LESSON 3 – *s*

Previously taught letters: long *e, m*

Lesson focus word: *See*

Sign Description

Draw the *s* shape in the air while making the *s* sound. Making the *s* shape with all fingers extended allows for smoother blending and word formation than drawing with the index finger only.

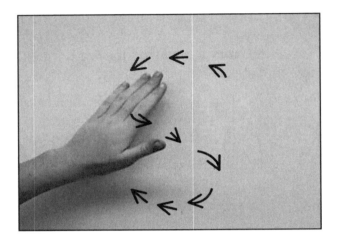

Procedures

1. Demonstrate the *s* sign.

2. Instruct students to make the *s* sound as they sign the letter.

3. Review the *e* sign and the word *me.*

4. Demonstrate blending the letter signs for *s* and *e* to form the word *see.* (The *e* sign should be made only once when signing the word *see*, even though the letter *e* appears twice.)

Student Page – #3

TEXT: See me.

ILLUSTRATION: Draw a picture of yourself doing something exciting.

Extension Activities

PICTURE DICTIONARY: See LESSON 2.

WATER WRITING: Instruct students to slowly make the *s* sign as one child writes the letter *s* on the board using a paintbrush and water. Repeat with additional children water writing.

WORD CHALLENGE: Discuss the meaning of the word *seem* and demonstrate how it would be signed.

Enrichment Activities

STRING ART: Instruct students to draw a large letter *S* on a sheet of paper, then glue string over the shape.

SEE ME BOOKLET: Ask students to find magazine pictures of someone doing something exciting. Cover the face of the person in the magazine picture with a snapshot or self-portrait of the child's face. Students then glue the picture to the bottom half of a sheet of paper and write *See Me* across the top.

Student Take-Home Book – *See Me*

NOTES

LESSON 4 – *w*

Previously taught letters: long *e*, *m*, *s*

Lesson focus word: *We*

Sign Description

Extend the three middle fingers of your left hand upward to resemble the letter *w*. Draw the letter *w* on your fingers with a washable marker. Then place the tips of the extended fingers to your throat as you make the *w* sound.

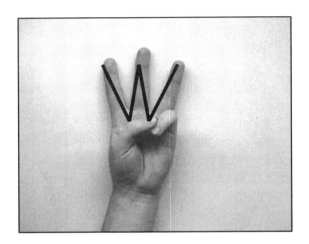 

Procedures

1. Demonstrate the *w* sign; instruct students to make the *w* sound as the sign is made.

2. Review the *e* sign.

3. Demonstrate blending the *w* sign with the *e* sign to form the word *we*.

Student Page – #4

TEXT: We see.

ILLUSTRATION: Draw a picture of yourself doing something exciting while two of your friends are watching.

Extension Activities

PICTURE DICTIONARY: Continue with each lesson (see LESSON 2).

WE OR *ME?* Make flash cards with the words *we* and *me* written in various sizes and colors. The students will sign the appropriate word when it is flashed.

WORD CHALLENGE (in this and subsequent lessons, allow students to tackle WORD CHALLENGE words independently before offering assistance; discuss word meanings as necessary): *wee.*

Enrichment Activities

3-D HANDS: Trace and cut out a silhouette of your left hand. Draw the letter *w* on the three middle fingers of your cutout. Roll the thumb and pinky to the back of your cutout, then glue the tips of these two fingers together, creating a 3-D representation of the *w* sign. Display on a board labeled "See What <u>We</u> Have Done."

SEASONAL SIGNS: Point out that the word *summer* begins with the letter *s* and the word *winter* begins with the letter *w*. Read a list of activities that might be performed during one of the two seasons. Students respond with the *w* sign for wintertime activities and with the *s* sign for summertime activities. Suggested activities might include making a snowman, swimming, building a fire in the fireplace, going barefoot, wearing a woolly coat, etc.

WE SEE BOOKLET: Make booklets similar to the *See Me* booklet described for LESSON 3, substituting the words "We See _____" and filling in the blank with the child's name.

Student Take-Home Book – *We See*

NOTES

LESSON 5 – short *u*

Previously taught letters: long *e, m, s, w*

Lesson focus word: *us*

Sign Description

Form the *u* shape with your left hand, as illustrated. Draw the shape of the letter on your hand with a washable marker. Touch your thumb to the underside of your chin while making the short-*u* sound.

Procedures

1. Demonstrate short-*u* sign, making the short-*u* sound as the sign is made.

2. Review the *s* sign.

3. Demonstrate blending the short-*u* and *s* signs to make the word *us.*

Student Page – #5

TEXT: See us.

ILLUSTRATION: Draw a picture of yourself having fun with two friends.

Extension Activities

WORD CHALLENGE (discuss plural forms of words): *mum, mums, muss, sum, sums* (approximate the *s* sound in the words *sums* and *mums*).

IT'S YOUR GUESS: Have students, one at a time, sign a WORD CHALLENGE word. Let other students guess the word that is being signed.

Enrichment Activities

SEE US BOOKLET: Follow the procedure for the *See Me* booklet (LESSON 3).

UMBRELLA *U*'s: Students will draw a large upper-case *U*, then invert the letter and embellish it to resemble an umbrella. Discuss the *u* sound at the beginning of the word *umbrella.*

Student Take-Home Book – *See Us*

NOTES

LESSON 6 – long *i*

Previously taught letters: long *e, m, s, w,* short *u*

Lesson focus word: *I* (as a word)

Sign Description

Draw the letter *i* on your index finger with a washable marker. Point to your left eye, with your index finger pointing straight upward, and then extend your hand forward while making the long-*i* sound.

Procedures

1. Demonstrate the long-*i* sign, making the long-*i* sound as the sign is made.

2. Review the *s* and long-*e* signs and the word *see.*

Student Page – #6

TEXT: I see …

ILLUSTRATION: Draw a picture of yourself looking at something behind a rock. Your friends are waiting for you to tell them what you see.

Extension Activities

I SEE YOU: One student at a time stands in front of the room with the words *I see* written over his/her head on the board. The class in unison signs *I see* _____, filling in the blank with the child's name.

WORD CHALLENGE: *mime, wise* (approximate the *s* sound in the word *wise).*

Enrichment Activity

"I See ..." (played similarly to "I Spy"). One child will sign the words *I see,* then end the sentence with a description of something he/she sees as the others guess the identity of the object.

Student Take-Home Book – *I See*

NOTES

LESSON 7 – *b*

Previously taught letters: long *e, m, s, w,* short *u,* long *i*

Lesson focus word: *bees*

Sign Description

Make a straight line with your left hand and a circle with your right hand, as illustrated. Explain that the straight line represents a baseball bat. Gently strike the *bat* against the *ball* while making the *b* sound. Remove your right hand but continue the same batting motion with the left hand. Explain that in the future only the left hand (the straight-line portion of the *b*) will be used to make the sign. This left hand will strike an imaginary ball. (Emphasize that the straight line in the letter *b* comes before the circle. This helps the children to differentiate more easily between the *b* and the *d*.)

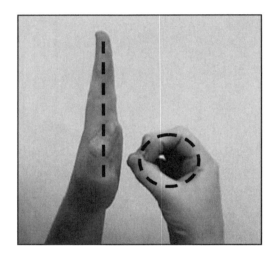

(initial presentation)

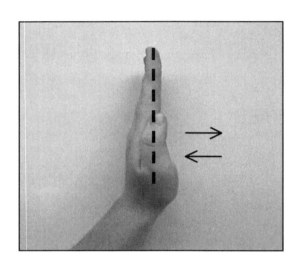

(actual *b* sign)

Procedures

1. Demonstrate the *b* sign; make the *b* sound as the sign is made.

2. Review the *e* and *s* signs; blend to make the word *bees.* Comment that the letter *s* sounds slightly different in the word *bees* from how it sounds in the word *see.*

3. Discuss *bees.*

Student Page – #7

TEXT: bees!

ILLUSTRATION: Draw a picture of bees flying over your head.

Extension Activities

BOARD WRITING (extension activities for the letter *b* should emphasize the fact that the straight line is written before the circle): Have two students go to the board. The first student draws the straight line, while the second student makes the *b* sign. The teacher or another child adds the circle to complete the letter *b*.

WORD CHALLENGE: *bum, bums, bus, sub, subs*

Enrichment Activity

HANDPRINTS: Brush finger paints onto the outside of the child's hand. The child presses the painted side of his/her hand to a sheet of paper, making the straight-line portion of the letter *b*. The circle can be added with a paintbrush, marker, printing tool, etc.

Student Take-Home Book – *Bees See*

NOTES

LESSON 8 – *n* (and silent *e*)

Previously taught letters: long *e*, *m*, *s*, *w*, short *u*, long *i*, *b*

Lesson focus word: *Nine*

Sign Description

Extend the index and middle fingers of your left hand downward, as illustrated in Step 1. Draw the letter *n* on the fingers with a washable marker. Place the tips of the extended fingers on your chin (Step 2). Pull downward on the chin slightly to emphasize the parting of your lips as you make the *n* sound.

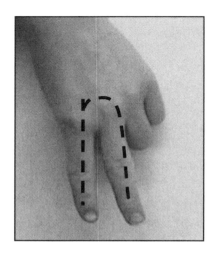

Procedures

1. Demonstrate the *n* sign, making the *n* sound as the sign is made.

2. Review the word *bees* and the long-*i* sound.

3. Explain the silent-*e* concept. When a silent *e* is encountered, students can place their right hand over their left fist to symbolize that the *e* is silent.

4. Demonstrate blending the *n*, long-*i*, *n*, and silent-*e* sounds to make the word *nine*.

Student Page – #8

TEXT: Nine bees …

ILLUSTRATION: Draw a picture of nine bees.

Extension Activities

WORD CHALLENGE: *bun, buns, mine, nub, nubs, nun, nuns, seen, sun, suns, swine, wine*

CHALK SPELLING: Slowly sign and pronounce words previously covered as the students write the words on individual chalkboards. When finished writing, each child holds up his/her board to be checked.

Enrichment Activity

NINE PICTURES: Instruct students to clip nine pictures of a particular object, such as nine cars, trees, etc. Then direct students to glue the pictures to a page labeled "Nine _____." Write the word that names their pictures in the blank for them, pointing out any previously covered letters.

Student Take-Home Book – *Nine Swine*

NOTES

for n sound you can put fingers
on your nose

LESSON 9 – *z*

Previously taught letters: long *e*, *m*, *s*, *w*, short *u*, long *i*, *b*, *n* (and silent *e*)

Lesson focus word: *buzz*

Sign Description

Draw the *z* shape in the air with your left hand, as illustrated.

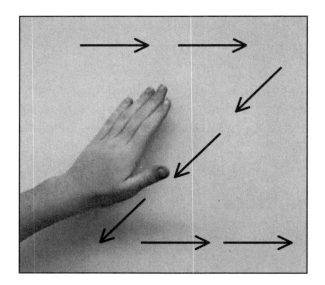

Procedures

1. Demonstrate the *z* sign, making the *z* sound as the sign is made.

2. Review the *b* and *u* signs.

3. Demonstrate blending the *b*, *u*, and *z* signs to make the word *buzz*.

Student Page – #9

TEXT: buzz.

ILLUSTRATION: Draw a picture of some bees, then write the word *buzz* beside each one.

Extension Activity

SLOW RACE: Conduct a <u>race</u> to see who can draw the letter *z* in the air the slowest, while making the *z* sound. Call time after one minute. Anyone who is still drawing the letter *z* and making the *z* sound when time is called is a winner.

Enrichment Activities

BUZZ: Read a list of words. When the students hear a word that begins with the letter *z*, they should make the *z* sign and sound. *Z* words might include *zeal, zebra, zenith, zero, zest, zigzag, zip, ZIP code, zipper, zodiac, zone, zoo,* and *zoom.*

ZZZZZ: Instruct students to find magazine pictures of people sleeping. Have them clip and glue the pictures to a sheet of paper. Explain that when some people snore they sometimes make a *z* sound. Instruct your students to draw several letter *z*'s over the picture of the sleeping person.

Student Take-Home Book – *Buzz, Buzz, Buzz*

NOTES

LESSON 10 – *r*

Previously taught letters: long *e, m, s, w,* short *u,* long *i, b, n* (and silent *e*), *z*

Lesson focus word: *Run*

Sign Description

Draw a large lower-case *r* on the board. Trace the curved portion of the *r* with your left hand, as illustrated, while making the *r* sound.

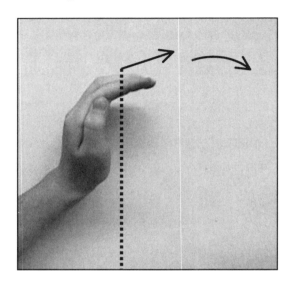

Procedures

1. Demonstrate the *r* sign, making the *r* sound as the sign is made.

2. Review the *u* and *n* signs.

3. Demonstrate blending the *r, u,* and *n* signs and sounds to make the word *run.*

Student Page – #10

Note: Introduce the upper-case R *before presenting the student page.*

TEXT: Run, run!

ILLUSTRATION: Draw a picture of you and your friends running away from the bees.

Extension Activities

CHEERS: Discuss cheering at a ballgame. In cheerleader style call out, "Give me an (make the *r* sign and sound)." The children will respond with the *r* sign and sound. Repeat for a *u* and an *n*. Then ask, "What did I spell?" Repeat the procedure for previously covered words.

WORD CHALLENGE: *rise, rub, rubs*

Enrichment Activity

RAINBOW *R*'s: Point out that the top part of the letter *r* (the part that is drawn when signing the letter) is shaped like a rainbow. Instruct the children to clip *r* words from magazines or newspapers and glue them to the rainbow-shaped portion of a large letter *r*.

Student Take-Home Book – *Nine Rats*

NOTES

LESSON 11 – *p*

Previously taught letters: long *e, m, s, w,* short *u,* long *i, b, n* (and silent *e*), *z, r*

Lesson focus word: *up*

Sign Description

Form a *p* shape with your left hand, as illustrated. Draw the letter *p* on your hand with a washable marker. Place the circular portion of the letter *p* in front of your lips as you make the *p* sound.

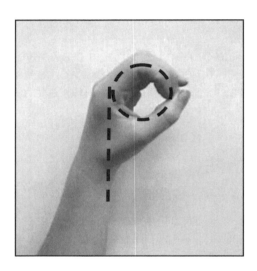 

Procedures

1. Demonstrate the *p* sign while making the *p* sound.

2. Review the *u* sign.

3. Demonstrate blending the *u* and *p* signs to make the word *up.*

Student Page – #11

TEXT: Run up!

ILLUSTRATION: Draw a picture of you and your friends running up a hill.

Extension Activities

WORD CHALLENGE: *bump, peep, peeps, pine, pipe, pipes, prime, prize, pump, pup, pups, ripe, weep, weeps, wipe*

LINE UP: Write each letter of the word *pipe* on an individual index card. Call four students to the front of the room and give each student one card. Line up the students so their cards will spell *pipe*. Without telling the word, have the first student make the *p* sign (sound included), the next make the long-*i* sign, the next make the *p* sign, and the last put his/her right hand over the left hand to represent the silent *e*. Let the class guess the word. Repeat the procedure for additional WORD CHALLENGE words.

PIPE-CLEANER *P*'s: Instruct students to make large *p* shapes using pipe cleaners. As you read a list of words, students use the pipe-cleaner *p*'s rather than their hands to make the *p* sign and sound when they hear a word that begins with the letter *p*.

Enrichment Activities

PLEASE PASS THE *P*'s: Students will glue dried peas to an outline of the letter *p*. Label the display "Please Pass the *P*'s."

GUESS THE *P* WORD: One student leaves the room while the rest of the class selects an object in the room that begins with the letter *p*. The excused student returns and walks around the room. The remaining students make the *p* sign (and sound) softly when the student is far away from the selected object – and loudly when he/she is close to it – until the object is identified.

Student Take-Home Book – *Pup*

NOTES

LESSON 12 – long *o*

> **Previously taught letters:** long *e, m, s, w,* short *u,* long *i, b, n* (and silent *e*), *z, r, p*
>
> **Lesson focus word:** *no*

Sign Description

Form an *o* shape with the left hand, as illustrated. Then extend your hand outward while making the long-*o* sound.

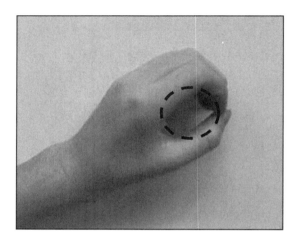 

Procedures

1. Demonstrate the long-*o* sign, making the long-*o* sound as the sign is made.

2. Review the *n* sign.

3. Demonstrate blending the *n* and *o* signs to make the word *no.*

Student Page – #12

Note: *Discuss the upper-case* N *before presenting the student page.*

TEXT: I see no bees.

ILLUSTRATION: Draw a picture of you and your friends at the top of the hill. You are happy because there are no bees there.

Extension Activities

WORD CHALLENGE: *bone, more, nose, or, pope, pose, robe, rope, rose, so, sore, wore, zone*

MORE *OR*s: Explain that the *or* sound is found in many words and should be recognized and signed fluently as a word chunk. Direct the students to sign the *or* portion of the following words quickly and fluently, as a word chunk rather than as two separate letters: *bore, more, nor, or, pore, sore, wore.*

YES/NO GAME: Ask a series of yes/no questions. Students will <u>sign</u> *no* or <u>say</u> *yes* in response to the questions.

Enrichment Activities

CHEERIO: List the WORD CHALLENGE words on the board. Give each child a small handful of Cheerios. Instruct them to write WORD CHALLENGE words, using cereal for the letter *o.*

E-I-E-I-O: Sing "Old McDonald," signing the *e, i, e, i, o* portion of the song.

Student Take-Home Book – *Sore Pup*

NOTES

LESSON 13 – long *a*

Previously taught letters: long *e, m, s, w,* short *u,* long *i, b, n* (and silent *e*), *z, r, p,* long *o*

Lesson focus word: *a* (as a word)

Sign Description

Rotate your hand in a counter-clockwise direction as if repeatedly tracing the circular part of the letter *a* with the palm of your hand while making the long-*a* sound. (A counter-clockwise direction should be followed because this is the direction used for writing the letter *a*.) The sign for the long-*a* sound should be made with the left arm extended outward, away from your body.

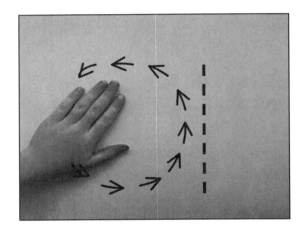

Procedures

1. Demonstrate the long-*a* sign, making the long-*a* sound as the sign is made.

2. Review the words *I* and *see.* Sign and read the word *pup* with the class. Discuss the meaning of the word *pup* as an abbreviated form of *puppy.*

Student Page – #13

TEXT: I see a pup.

ILLUSTRATION: Draw a picture of a puppy.

Extension Activities

CHART ART: Explain that the long-*a* sign is the same way for all spellings. Make a chart listing other common ways to spell the long-*a* sound. (This activity should be repeated for other vowel sounds at the appropriate time.)

Long *a*	
<u>ai</u>	*<u>ay</u>*
brain	bay
drain	may
main	pray
pain	ray
rain	say

WORD CHALLENGE: *ape, bare, base, bay, brain, drain, main, mane, mare, may, name, pain, pane, pare, pray, rain, ray, same, sane, say, Zane*

Enrichment Activity

WHAT DO YOU SEE?   Write the words "I see a _____" on the board. Ask questions, such as "What do you see that is blue?" One student will sign *I see a _____*, then fill in the blank with something he/she sees that is blue.

Student Take-Home Book – *Zane*

NOTES

LESSON 14 – *h*

Previously taught letters: long *e, m, s, w,* short *u,* long *i, b, n* (and silent *e*), *z, r, p,* long *o,* long *a*

Lesson focus word: *Hi*

Sign Description

Shape your left hand to resemble the letter *h*, as illustrated. Draw an *h* on your hand with a washable marker. Then position your hand in front of your mouth as you make the *h* sound.

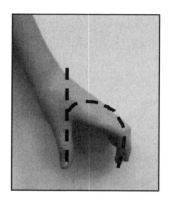 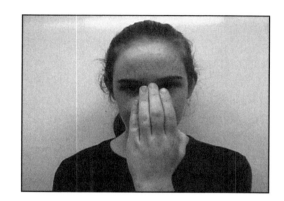

Procedures

1. Demonstrate the *h* sign, making the *h* sound as the sign is made.

2. Review the *i* sign.

3. Demonstrate blending the *h* and *i* signs to make the word *hi*.

Student Page – #14

Note: Introduce upper-case H *before beginning the student page.*

TEXT: Hi, pup.

ILLUSTRATION: Draw a picture of yourself petting the pup.

Extension Activities

WORD CHALLENGE: *hay, he, hoe, ho-hum, home, homes, hope, hose, hub, hump, humps*

FILL-IN-THE-BLANKS LISTENING ACTIVITY (read the following list of words, omitting the beginning *h* sound; students will add the *h* sign and sound and pronounce the word): *hair, hall, halo, ham, hammer, hamster, hand, hang, happy, hard, harm, harp, hat, he, head, hear, heart, heat, hello, help, her, hiccup, high, hill, hog, hold, home, honey, hop, hope, horn, horse, hose, hot, house, hungry, hunt, hum* and *hurry.*

Enrichment Activity

HI HO, HI HO: Sing the "Snow White" song … *Hi ho, hi ho; it's off to work we go.* Students will make the *h* sign whenever they hear the *h* sound. Following the song, students may sign the words *hi* and *ho.*

Student Take-Home Book – *Pup Sees*

NOTES

LESSON 15 – *y* (long *i*)

Previously taught letters: long *e, m, s, w*, short *u*, long *i, b, n* (and silent *e*), *z, r, p*, long *o*, long *a, h*
Lesson focus word: *my*

Sign Description

Draw an imaginary *y* shape on your thumb, index finger, and palm. Point to your eye **with your index finger, then extend your hand forward while making the long-*i* sound.**

show letter looks like Y a point to eye
start with y end up with long eye

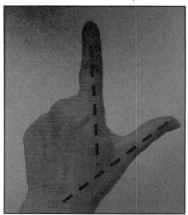

Procedures

1. Demonstrate the *y* sign; make the long-*i* sound as the sign is made.

2. Review the *m* sign.

3. Demonstrate blending the *m* and *y* signs to make the word *my*.

Student Page – #15

TEXT: I see my horse.

ILLUSTRATION: Draw a picture of you and your horse.

Extension Activities

MY, MY, MY: Students show something that belongs to them as they sign *my* and then name the object they are showing.

WORD CHALLENGE: *by, pry*

BY WHOM? Instruct students to write the word *by* in front of their name on their paper.

Enrichment Activities

MY _____: Students will draw a picture of something that belongs to them and label the picture "My _____" (naming the object in the blank).

OR WHAT? Point out the *or* sound in the word *horse.* Practice signing the word *or* until it becomes automatic. Remind students that *or* should be signed as a unit when encountered in words.

Student Take-Home Book – *Mine, Mine, Mine!*

NOTES

LESSON 16 – *d*

Previously taught letters: long *e, m, s, w,* short *u,* long *i, b, n* (and silent *e*), *z, r, p,* long *o,* long *a, h, y* (long-*i* sound)

Lesson focus word: *Ride*

Sign Description

Form an *o* shape with your left hand. For the purpose of introducing the sign, also make a stick shape with the right hand. Explain that the *o* shape (left hand) represents a dog digging under a fence post (right hand). Make a circular digging motion with your left hand, as illustrated. Explain that in the future only the left hand (the circular, digging portion of the *d)* will be used to make the *d* sign.

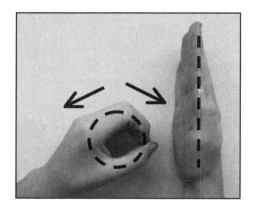

(initial presentation)

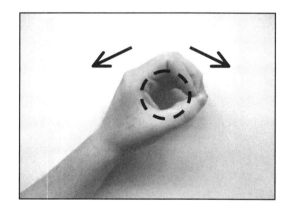

(actual *d* sign)

Procedures

1. Demonstrate the *d* sign and make the *d* sound as the sign is made.

2. Review the *r* and long-*i* signs, as well as the silent-*e* concept.

3. Demonstrate blending the *r,* long-*i,* and *d* signs to make the word *ride*.

Student Page – #16

TEXT: Ride my horse.

ILLUSTRATION: Draw a picture of you and your friends riding your horse.

Extension Activities

Note: *In order to help students differentiate between the* b *and the* d, *it's important for extension activities to emphasize the fact that the circular, digging portion of the letter* d *is written first.*

DIGGING UP *D*'s: Bury items that begin with the letter *d* in a sand bucket. Allow students to dig for and identify each item, making the *d* sign as each item is named.

WORD CHALLENGE: *bud, dame, day, deem, deep, dime, dine, doe, drape* (chunk the *dr* in *drape*) *drum, dump, hide, made, mud, rode, seed, side, suds, wade, weed, wide*

Enrichment Activity

DONUTS AND CARROTS (instruct the students to wash their hands before beginning this activity): Give each child a paper towel, a donut, and a carrot. Students will arrange the donut and the carrot on the paper towel to form a *d* shape. Emphasize the fact that the donut (which they probably like better) comes before the carrot and that the donut begins with the *d* sound. Allow students to eat their letter *d* after they have made the *d* sign.

Student Take-Home Book – *My Horse Runs*

NOTES

LESSON 17 – *g*

> **Previously taught letters:** long *e, m, s, w,* short *u,* long *i, b, n* (and silent *e*), *z, r, p,* long *o,* long *a, h, y* (long-*i* sound), *d*
>
> **Lesson focus word:** *go*

Note: The hard g *is presented in this lesson.* The soft-g *sound is discussed in the Appendix.*

Sign Description

Curl the fingers of your left hand to form a *g* shape, as illustrated. Place your hand against your throat to feel the guttural vibrations while making the hard-*g* sound.

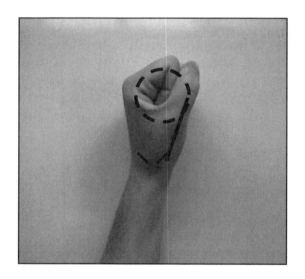 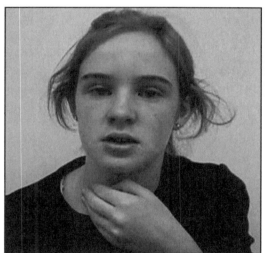

Procedures

1. Demonstrate the *g* sign, making the hard-*g* sound as the sign is made.

2. Review the long-*o* sign.

3. Demonstrate blending the *g* and *o* signs to make the word *go.*

Student Page – #17

TEXT: See us go.

ILLUSTRATION: Draw a picture of your horse running.

Extension Activity

WORD CHALLENGE: *bug, dug, game, gape, grade, grain, grape, gray, greed, gripe, grub, grump, gum, Gus, hug, mug, rug*

Enrichment Activities

G SONG (sung to the tune of "Twinkle, Twinkle, Little Star"):

> Curl your thumb, and you will see
> You have made the letter *g*.
> Put your *g* up to your throat,
> Then say words like *g-g-goat*.
> You can feel that hard-*g* sound
> Every time the *g* comes 'round.

LOOKING UP: Students lie on their backs, make the *g* sign, and repeat words pronounced by the teacher that contain the hard-*g* sound.

Student Take-Home Book – *Gray Bug*

NOTES

LESSON 18 – *j*

> **Previously taught letters:** long *e, m, s, w,* short *u,* long *i, b, n* (and silent *e*), *z, r, p,* long *o,* long *a, h, y* (long-*i* sound), *d, g*
>
> **Lesson focus word:** *jump*

Sign Description

Draw the *j* shape in the air with the index finger of your left hand while making the *j* sound.

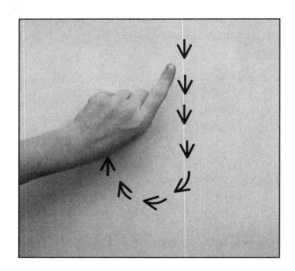

Procedures

1. Demonstrate the *j* sign, making the *j* sound as the sign is made.

2. Review the *u, m,* and *p* signs.

3. Demonstrate blending the *j, u, m,* and *p* signs to make the word *jump.*

Student Page – #18

TEXT: See us jump.

ILLUSTRATION: Draw a picture of your horse jumping over something.

Extension Activities

WORD CHALLENGE: *jade, Jane, Jay, Jeep, Jo, Joe, jug*

JUMPING-*J* RELAY: Divide the class into teams for a relay. The first person on each team must jump from the team's starting point to its destination point and back. Each child must make the *j* sign and sound with each jump.

Enrichment Activity

JIGGLERS: Make Jell-o jigglers for snack.

Student Take-Home Book – *Little Girls*

NOTES

LESSON 19 – *f*

> **Previously taught letters:** long *e, m, s, w,* short *u,* long *i, b, n* (and silent *e*), *z, r, p,* long *o,* long *a, h, y* (long-*i* sound), *d, g, j*
>
> **Lesson focus word:** *Fun*

Sign Description

Draw the letter *f* on your left hand with a washable marker, as illustrated. Place your hand in front of your lips while making the *f* sound.

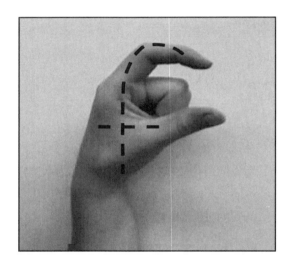

Procedures

1. Demonstrate the *f* sign, making the *f* sound as the sign is made.

2. Review the *u* and *n* signs.

3. Demonstrate blending the *f, u,* and *n* signs to make the word *fun.*

Student Page – #19

Note: Introduce the upper-case F *before beginning the student page.*

TEXT: Fun, fun, fun.

ILLUSTRATION: Draw a picture of you and your friends smiling as you ride your horse.

Extension Activities

WORD CHALLENGE: *fade, fame, fee, feed, find, fine, for, frame, fray, freed, freeze, fry, fuss, fuzz*

SLOW RACE: Have a <u>race</u> to see who can be the last to finish making the *f* sign (and *f* sound). Call time after 30 seconds. All students still making the *f* sound when time is called are winners.

FE, FI, FO, FUM: Read "Jack and the Beanstalk." Students can sign *Fe, Fi, Fo, Fum* when it is read.

Enrichment Activity

FAVORITE THINGS: Play a recording of the song "My Favorite Things" (from *The Sound of Music*). Direct the class in rewriting the song to contain favorite things that begin with the letter *f.* For example:

Footballs and fossils and feathers and faces,
Foxes and Frisbees and fantastic places,
French fries and fiddles and farm bells that ring …
These are a few of my favorite things.

Student Take-Home Book – *Fe, Fi, Fo, Fum*

NOTES

LESSON 20 – *t*

> **Previously taught letters:** long *e, m, s, w,*
> short *u,* long *i, b, n* (and silent *e*), *z, r, p,*
> long *o,* long *a, h, y* (long-*i* sound), *d, g, j, f*
>
> **Lesson focus word:** *Time*

Sign Description

Make the horizontal portion of the *t* shape with the index finger of your left hand, as illustrated, then make the vertical portion with the right hand. Gently tap the two fingers together while making the *t* sound. Remove the right hand. Explain that in the future only the left hand (the horizontal portion of the *t)* will be used to make the sign, as the index finger of the left hand strikes an <u>imaginary</u> vertical portion of the *t.*

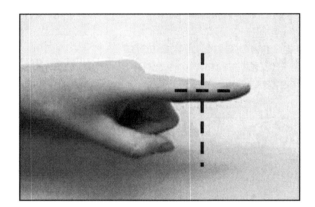

Procedures

1. Demonstrate the *t* sign, making the *t* sound as the sign is made.

2. Review the long-*i* and *m* signs, as well as the silent-*e* concept.

3. Demonstrate blending the *t*, *i*, and *m* signs to make the word *time.*

Student Page – #20

TEXT: Time for ...

ILLUSTRATION: Draw a picture of you and your friends sitting on the ground beside your horse.

Extension Activities

WORD CHALLENGE: *beet, bite, but, date, fate, feet, gate, hate, hut, just, jut, mate, meet, note, nut, rate, rust, rut, stain, state, stay, stone, store, street, stride, tame, tape, teen, tide, tone, tore, trade, train, tray, trust, tub, tug*

TAMBOURINE TIME: Obtain tambourines for as many of your students as possible. Read a list of words as the children march around the room, striking the tambourine when they hear a word that begins with *t.*

TOOTHPICK *T*'s: Students will make *t* shapes with toothpicks, then use a marker to complete a word beginning with the letter *t.*

Enrichment Activity

T-SHIRTS: Students may decorate cutout T-shirt shapes with pictures of objects that begin with the letter *t.*

Student Take-Home Book – *Gus*

NOTES

LESSON 21 – short *a*

> **Previously taught letters:** long *e, m, s, w,* short *u,* long *i, b, n* (and silent *e*), *z, r, p,* long *o,* long *a, h, y* (long-*i* sound), *d, g, j, f, t*
>
> **Lesson focus word:** *nap*

Sign Description

The sign for the short-*a* sound is the same as for the long *a*, except the sign should be made at eye level rather than at chest level.

Procedures

1. Demonstrate the short-*a* sign, making the short-*a* sound as the sign is made.

2. Review the *n* and *p* signs.

3. Demonstrate blending the *n*, short *a*, and *p* signs to make the word *nap*.

Student Page – #21

TEXT: a nap.

ILLUSTRATION: Draw a picture of you and your friends sleeping.

Extension Activities

WORD CHALLENGE: *am, bad, bag, ban, band, bat, brass, dad, Dan, drab, drag, fan, fast, fat, gag, gap, gas, grab, grass, had, hand, hat, jam, lag, mad, man, map, mass, mat, Nan, pad, pan, past, pat, rag, ram, ran, rap, rat, sad, sag, Sam, sat, Stan, tap, tram, trap, wag, zap*

LONG *A*/SHORT *A:* Read a list of words that contain either the long-*a* or short-*a* sound. Students will respond with appropriate long- or short-*a* sign.

Enrichment Activities

A WHEELS: Students may make a word wheel of the *at* word family.

SHORT-*A* POEM (sung to the tune of "Three Blind Mice"):

> That fat cat,
> That fat cat.
> Sat on my hat,
> Sat on my hat.
> He sat on my hat, and he mashed it flat,
> Then chased a rat with a baseball bat.
> Have you ever heard of a cat like that?
> That fat cat!

WHAT SAT ON WHAT? Instruct students to complete and illustrate the sentence, "A _____ sat on a _____," using words that end with *at.*

Student Take-Home Book – *Bad Nan*

NOTES

LESSON 22 – *k*

Previously taught letters: long *e, m, s, w,* short *u,* long *i, b, n* (and silent *e*), *z, r, p,* long *o,* long *a, h, y* (long-*i* sound), *d, g, j, f, t,* short *a*

Lesson focus word: *Wake*

Sign Description

Draw the *k* shape on your hand with a washable marker, as illustrated. Make the hard-*k* sound while doing a cutting motion with your index finger and forefinger.

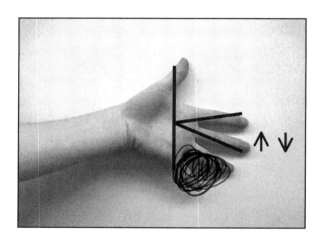

Procedures

1. Demonstrate the *k* sign, making the *k* sound as the sign is made.

2. Review the *w* and long-*a* signs, as well as the silent-*e* concept.

3. Demonstrate blending the *w,* long-*a,* and *k* and silent *e* signs to make the word *wake.*

4. Introduce the sight-word concept and the sight word *to.*

Student Page – #22

TEXT: Wake up! Wake up! Time to go home.

ILLUSTRATION: Draw a picture of you and your friends awake.

© Bethanie H. Tucker • **aha!** Process, Inc. • (800) 424-9484

Extension Activities

CUTTING *K*'s: Cut the fingers from discarded pairs of gloves. Give two <u>fingers</u> to each child who will slip them over the index and middle fingers to resemble a pair of scissors. The students will make the *k* sign with their <u>scissors fingers</u> each time you read a word that beings with the *k* sound.

WORD CHALLENGE: *awake, bake, bike, bunk, fake, fork, hike, hunk, Jake, junk, Kay, keen, keep, kid, kind, kite, make, Mike, musk, peek, pike, poke, rake, sake, sky, snake, spike, stake, strike, stripe, take*

Enrichment Activity

K KITES: Write on the board a list of words that begin with the letter *k*. Students may clip magazine pictures of the listed objects and glue them to a large class-sized kite.

Student Take-Home Book – *Kay Pokes*

NOTES

LESSON 23 – c

Previously taught letters: long *e, m, s, w,* short *u,* long *i, b, n* (and silent *e*), *z, r, p,* long *o,* long *a, h, y* (long-*i* sound), *d, g, j, f, t,* short *a, k*

Lesson focus word: *can*

Sign Description

The hand position for the hard-*c* sound is the same as for the *k* (see LESSON 22). Point out that the letter *c* is "hidden" inside the letter *k*. The vertical line, however, should not be drawn.

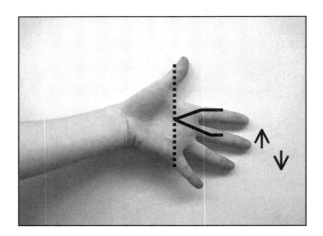

Procedures

1. Demonstrate the hard-*c* sign, making the *k* sound as the sign is made.

2. Review the short-*a* and *n* signs.

3. Demonstrate blending the *c*, short *a*, and *n* signs to make the word *can*.

Student Page – #23

TEXT: My horse can run fast.

ILLUSTRATION: Draw a picture of your horse running fast.

Extension Activities

WORD CHALLENGE: *cab, cake, came, cane, cap, cape, care, carp, case, cast, cat, code, comb, cone, cope, core, crab, cram, crane, crate, creed, creep, crime, crust, cry, cub, cup*

CK CAN TOO: Explain that the hard-*c* sound is sometimes spelled *ck.* WORD CHALLENGE words for the *ck* spelling include *back, buck, crack, hack, jack, Mack, pack, rack, sack, stack, struck, stuck, tack, track, truck,* and *Zack.*

REPEAT "CUTTING *K*'s" (see LESSON 22), calling this activity "CUTTING *C*'s."

Enrichment Activity

CRAZY CAKE: List words on the board that begin with the hard-*c* sound. Students may list ingredients for a *crazy cake,* choosing ingredients from the list of words on the board. Students may draw a picture of their *crazy cakes.*

Student Take-Home Book – *Can I Find?*

NOTES

LESSON 24 – *L*

> **Previously taught letters:** long *e, m, s, w,* short *u,* long *i, b, n* (and silent *e*), *z, r, p,* long *o,* long *a, h, y* (long-*i* sound), *d, g, j, f, t,* short *a, k, c*
>
> **Lesson focus word:** *last*

Sign Description

Glide through the shape of the upper-case letter *L* with the left hand, as illustrated, while making the *L* sound. (The upper-case *L* shape is used for the *L* sign because it is more easily recognizable than the lower-case *l*.)

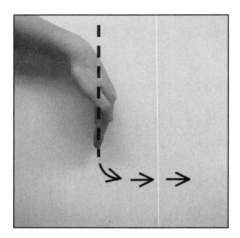

Procedures

1. Demonstrate the *L* sign, making the *L* sound as the sign is made.

2. Review the short-*a, s,* and *t* signs.

3. Demonstrate blending the *L, a, s,* and *t* signs to make the word *last.*

4. Explain that the upper- and lower-case letters are signed the same way.

Student Page – #24

TEXT: Home at last.

ILLUSTRATION: Draw a picture of you and your friends at your house.

Extension Activities

WORD CHALLENGE: *Bill, bleed, clam, clan, close, eel, flake, fleet, glad, hill, lab, lad, lame, lane, lap, late, leek, like, line, lug, pile, pill, sleep, slide, slime, stale*

LAZY *L:* Explain that the *L* makes a lazy sound. Students can *lazily* make the *L* sign and exaggerate the *L* sound as they repeat words beginning with *L* that you read.

Enrichment Activity

LUCY LOVED HER LITTLE LAMB (sing the following song to the tune of "Mary Had a Little Lamb," making the *L* sign as each *L* is pronounced):

> Lucy loved her little lamb, little lamb, little lamb;
> Lucy loved her little lamb; its legs were long and low.
> Everywhere that Lucy went, Lucy went, Lucy went,
> Everywhere that Lucy went, the lamb was sure to go.

Student Take-Home Book – *Lee Likes*

NOTES

LESSON 25 – short *I*

Previously taught letters: long *e, m, s, w,* short *u,* long *i, b, n* (and silent *e*), *z, r, p,* long *o,* long *a, h, y* (long-*i* sound), *d, g, j, f, t,* short *a, k, c, L*

Lesson focus words: *pig, pink, big, it, is*

Sign Description

Make the same sign as for the long *i*, except the index finger should be held horizontally, as illustrated. Make the short-*i* sound as the sign is made.

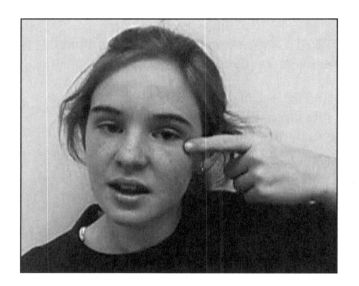

Procedures

1. Demonstrate the short-*i* sign, making the short-*i* sound as the sign is made.

2. Review the *p* and *g* signs.

3. Demonstrate blending the *p, i,* and *g* signs to make the word *pig*. Repeat for *pink, big, it,* and *is.*

Student Page – #25

TEXT: I see a pig. It is a pink pig, and it is big.

ILLUSTRATION: Draw a picture of a pig.

Extension Activities

WORD CHALLENGE: *bid, bin, bit, bliss, brim, clip, did, dig, dim, dip, drill, fig, fill, fin, fit, fizz, flip, frill, grid, grin, grit, hid, him, hip, hit, ill, in, Jill, Jim, kick, kid, kill, Kim, kin, kiss, kit, lid, lip, mill, miss, mitt, pick, pin, pit, rib, Rick, rip, sick, sin, sip, sis, sit, slick, slid, slim, slit, stiff, still, swim, tick, Tim, tin, tip, trick, trim, trip, wig, will, win, wit*

PICK A CARD: One student at a time goes to the front of the room and signs a word from the list above. The student who correctly guesses the word gets to sign the next one.

LONG *I*/SHORT *I*: Read a list of words that contain either the long-*i* or the short-*i* sound. Students respond with the appropriate *i* sign.

SPELL WELL: The teacher slowly reads and signs a short word that contains the short-*i* sound. On individual chalkboards or tablets, students write the word being signed, then hold up their chalkboards/tablets so the teacher can see when they've finished writing the word.

Enrichment Activity

THE SHORT-*I* GAME: On the playground one child in a group of about 10 students is designated "it." In order to avoid being tagged and becoming "it," the other students must call out a word that contains the short-*i* sound while making the short-*i* sign. Words may not be repeated.

Student Take-Home Book – *Big Bad Pig*

NOTES

LESSON 26 – short *e*

Previously taught letters: long *e, m, s, w,* short *u,* long *i, b, n* (and silent *e*), *z, r, p,* long *o,* long *a, h, y* (long-*i* sound), *d, g, j, f, t,* short *a, k, c, L,* short *i*

Lesson focus words: *pet, let, wet*

Sign Description

The sign for short *e* is made like the long-*e* sign, except the hand is held at eye level rather than at chest level. Make the short-*e* sound as the sign is made.

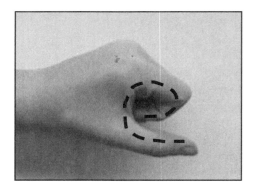 

Procedures

1. Demonstrate the short-*e* sign, making the short-*e* sound as the sign is made.

2. Review the *p, t, w,* and *L* signs.

3. Demonstrate blending the signs to make the words *pet, let,* and *wet.*

Student Page – #26

TEXT: It is my pet pig. I let my pet play in wet mud.

ILLUSTRATION: Draw a picture of your pet pig playing in the mud.

Extension Activities

WORD CHALLENGE: *bed, beg, bell, Ben, Bess, best, bet, bled, bless, deck, den, dress, fed, fell, fled, Fred, fret, hem, hen, Jed, jell, jest, jet, keg, led, leg, less, let, Meg, men, mess, met, neck, Ned, Nell, nest, net, peck, pen, pep, pled, press, rest, sell, set, sled, stem, step, swell, Ted, tell, ten, test, web, zest*

LONG *E*/SHORT *E:* Read a list of words that contain either the long *e* or the short *e* sound. Students respond by making the appropriate *e* sign.

MAKE-A-WORD: Write the following letters on individual index cards and distribute two cards to each student in the following combinations: *b & d; b & g; b & ll; b & t; d & ll; f & d; f & ll; g & t; L & g; L & t; m & g; m & t; n & t; p & g; p & n; p & p; p & t; r & d; s & ll, s & t; t & d; t & ll; t & n; v & t; w & d; w & t; w & ll;* and. Place an index card on which the letter *e* has been written in the chalk tray. One child at a time takes his/her cards to the board and places one card before the *e* and the other card after the *e* to make a word. The other students sign and read the completed word.

Enrichment Activity

SHORT-*E* PUZZLES: Put the cards used in the MAKE-A-WORD activity into individual Zip-lock bags and place them in an activity center. Allow each student in the center to make word puzzles by using the index cards to create words around a large letter *e* drawn in the center of a sheet of paper.

Student Take-Home Book – *A Big Egg*

NOTES

LESSON 27 – *sh*

Previously taught letters: long *e, m, s, w,* short *u,* long *i, b, n* (and silent *e*), *z, r, p,* long *o,* long *a, h, y* (long-*i* sound), *d, g, j, f, t,* short *a, k, c, L,* short *i,* short *e*

Lesson focus word: *She*

Sign Description

Hold your extended index finger vertically in front of your lips, as illustrated, while making the *sh* sound.

Procedures

1. Demonstrate the *sh* sign, making the *sh* sound as the sign is made.

2. Review the long-*e* sign.

3. Demonstrate blending the *sh* and *e* signs to make the word *she.*

Student Page – #27

TEXT: She is a mess.

ILLUSTRATION: Draw a picture of your pet pig covered with mud.

Extension Activities

WORD CHALLENGE: *brush, cash, crash, dash, dish, fish, flash, gash, sash, shack, shade, shame, shape, sheep, sheet, shelf, shell, shine, ship, shock, shore, short, trash*

S OR *SH*? As you read the following list of words, the students will make the sign of the beginning sound, either *s* or *sh: sell, see, she, same, sack, sad, shake, sake, sham, Sam, sheen, seen, seep, shelf, self, shift, sift, shin, sin, sip, sock, sort, shag,* and *sag.*

Enrichment Activities

HEAD AND SHOULDERS, SHOES AND SHINS (sing to the tune of "Head and Shoulders, Knees and Toes," pointing to the appropriate body part as each part is named):

> Head and shoulders, shoes and shins, shoes and shins,
> Head and shoulders, shoes and shins, shoes and shins;
> Our shirts and shorts and shampoo too (point to hair) …
> Head and shoulders, shoes and shins, shoes and shins.

SH-SH-SH-SH: Explain that the *sh* sound usually indicates a request for others to be very quiet. Instruct the students to sit quietly in a circle on the carpet and softly make the *sh* sound. One student at a time names a word that begins with *sh* until all students have responded.

Student Take-Home Book – *A Fish for a Sheep*

NOTES

LESSON 28 – *er/ir/ur*

> **Previously taught letters:** long *e, m, s, w,* short *u,* long *i, b, n* (and silent *e*), *z, r, p,* long *o,* long *a, h, y* (long-*i* sound), *d, g, j, f, t,* short *a, k, c, L,* short *i,* short *e, sh*
>
> **Lesson focus word:** *girl*

Sign Description

Rotate the index finger of your left hand in the air, as illustrated, while making the *er* sound. Move your finger in an upward spiral. Explain that the index finger is tw*ir*ling in the air.

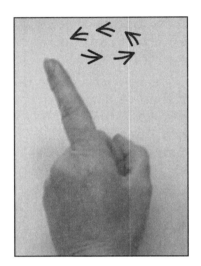 

Procedures

1. Demonstrate the *ir* sign, making the *ir* sound as the sign is make.

2. Review the *g* and *L* signs.

3. Demonstrate blending the *g, ir,* and *L* signs to make the word *girl.*

4. Introduce the sight word *one.*

Student Page – #28

TEXT: My pig is a girl. Her name is Furl. One day Furl ran away.

ILLUSTRATION: Draw a picture of your pet pig running away.

Extension Activities

WORD CHALLENGE: *Bert, bird, blurt, burn, burst, curb, curd, curt, dirt, fern, fir, firm, first, flirt, her, herd, hurl, hurt, jerk, lurk, nurse, perk, purr, purse, shirt, sir, stern, term, terse, turn, twirl*

WORD DETECTIVES: Tell the students that detectives look for clues to help them figure things out. Explain that they will be word detectives and look for such clues as *er, ir,* or *ur* to help them read words. Write a WORD CHALLENGE word on the board. Allow a student to circle with colored chalk the *e/i/u-r* combinations. The remainder of the students should make the *e/i/u-r* sign if the circle is drawn correctly. Slowly sign and read the word with the class. Repeat with additional WORD CHALLENGE words. (Exceptions such as *word* and *world* should be taught later as sight words.)

Enrichment Activity

BIRDS OF A FEATHER: Prepare a board containing pockets labeled *er, ir,* and *ur.* Pockets can be decorated to look like feathers. Print each of the words used in the WORD CHALLENGE, then place them in the appropriate pocket. Label the board "Birds of a Feather."

Student Take-Home Book – *Burt Flirts*

NOTES

LESSON 29 – short *o*

Previously taught letters: long *e, m, s, w,* short *u,* long *i, b, n* (and silent *e*), *z, r, p,* long *o,* long *a, h, y* (long-*i* sound), *d, g, j, f, t,* short *a, k, c, L,* short *i,* short *e, sh, er/ir/ur*

Lesson focus words: *got, hot*

Sign Description

Hold your left hand at eye level, make an *o* shape, as illustrated, then make the *o* sound.

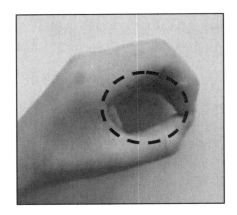 

Procedures

1. Demonstrate the short-*o* sign, making the short-*o* sound as the sign is made.

2. Review the *g, h,* and *t* signs.

3. Demonstrate blending the signs to make the words *got* and *hot.*

4. Introduce the sight word *was.*

Student Page – #29

TEXT: It was a summer day. My pig got hot. She went to sleep.

ILLUSTRATION: Draw a picture of your pet pig asleep.

Extension Activities

WORD CHALLENGE: *blob, block, blot, bog, bop, clock, clod, clog, clop, clot, cob, cod, cog, cop, cot, crock, crop, dock, dog, doll, Don, dot, drop, frog, gob, God, hog, hop, job, jog, Josh, jot, lock, log, lot, mob, mock, Mom, mop, not, odd, off, plod, plop, plot, pod, pop, pot, prod, prom, prop, rob, rock, rod, rot, shock, shod, shop, shot, slop, slosh, slot, sob, sock, sod, sop, stock, stop, Tom, top, tot*

WHAT DO YOU SEE? Write the following words on the board, signing and reading each word with the class. Allow students to make generalizations as to why certain words contain the short-*o* sound, while others contain long *o*: *cop, cope, dot, dote, hop, hope, mop, mope, not, note, rob, robe, rod, rode, tot,* and *tote.*

Enrichment Activity

MAGNETIC WORDS: Prepare two sets of magnetic letters, each set containing all of the previously taught consonants and the letter *o*. Place each set on a magnetic surface for the whole class to see. Read and sign a word containing the short *o*, allowing one student from each of two teams to race to rearrange the letters and spell the word. Repeat with additional words from the WORD CHALLENGE list.

Student Take-Home Book – *Mom Shops*

NOTES

LESSON 30 – *th*

Previously taught letters: long *e, m, s, w,* short *u,* long *i, b, n* (and silent *e*), *z, r, p,* long *o,* long *a, h, y* (long-*i* sound), *d, g, j, f, t,* short *a, k, c, L,* short *i,* short *e, sh, er/ir/ur,* short *o*

Lesson focus words: *thin, thick, with*

Sign Description

Pretend to touch the tip of your tongue with your index finger while making the *th* sound.

use thumb instead of index finger

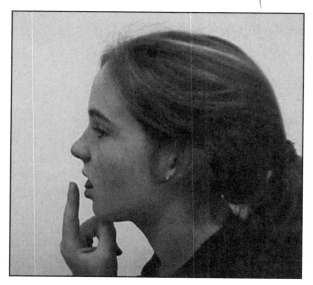

Procedures

1. Demonstrate the *th* sign, making the *th* sound as the sign is made.

2. Review the short-*i, n, ck,* and *w* signs.

3. Demonstrate blending the signs to make the words *thin, thick,* and *with*.

Student Page – #30

TEXT: A thin sheep with thick hair came by. The thin sheep sat by the pig.

ILLUSTRATION: Draw a picture of a thin sheep looking at the sleeping pig.

Extension Activity

WORD CHALLENGE: *Beth, both, path, than* (briefly point out the fact that *th* makes two sounds*), thank, that, then, think, third, thirst, this, thorn, those* (approximate the *s* sound*) thud, thump, thus, thy, with*

Enrichment Activity

YUMMY *TH:* Instruct all students to wash their hands thoroughly. Give each child a small quantity of pudding. At your signal all students dip the tip of his/her index finger of their left hand into the pudding. When someone thinks of a word that contains the *th* sound, he/she calls it out, then everyone says the word and touches his/her tongue while making the *th* sound. (Stress the fact that normally we do not actually touch our tongues to make this sign.)

Student Take-Home Book – *The Dog's Birthday*

NOTES

LESSON 31 – *ing*

Previously taught letters: long *e, m, s, w,* short *u,* long *i, b, n* (and silent *e), z, r, p,* long *o,* long *a, h, y* (long-*i* sound), *d, g, j, f, t,* short *a, k, c, L,* short *i,* short *e, sh, er/ir/ur,* short *o, th*

Lesson focus words: *going, sleeping*

Sign Description

Review the signs for short-*i, n,* and *g.* Demonstrate blending the three signs into one fluid motion; only hint at the *n* sign as your hand moves from the short-*i* to the *g* position. The *ing* sign becomes a single, rapid movement.

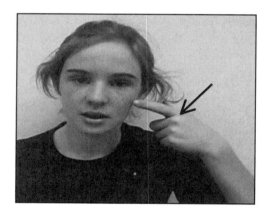 

Procedures

1. Demonstrate the *ing* sign, making the *ing* sound as the sign is made.

2. Review the *g,* long-*o, s, L, e,* and *p* signs.

3. Demonstrate blending the signs to make the words *going* and *sleeping.*

Student Page – #31

TEXT: But the pig kept sleeping, so the sheep got up and kept going.

ILLUSTRATION: Draw a picture of the sheep walking away.

Extension Activities

WORD CHALLENGE: *bagging, batting, betting, blasting, bleeding, blessing, blinding, blurting, brimming, bring, bringing, bumping, burning, capping, casting, clapping, cling, clipping, clothing, creeping, crying, curling, dashing, digging, dimming, ding, dinging, dipping, dragging, dressing, drilling, dropping, drumming, drying, fasting, feeding, filling, finding, fishing, flapping, fling, flinging, flirting, flunking, freeing, fretting, frying, fussing, going, grabbing, grinning, grubbing, grumping, hitting, hemming, hopping, hugging, humming, hurting, jerking, jogging, jumping, jutting, keeping, kicking, kidding, killing, king, kissing, lacking, lapping, laying, letting, logging, lumping, mapping, mashing, missing, mopping, napping, packing, passing, patting, paying, pecking, peeking, peeling, peeping, petting, ping, pinging, planning, playing, popping, praying, pressing, prying, pumping, ramming, resting, ring, ringing, robbing, rotting, rubbing, running, rusting, sagging, saying, seeing, seeding, seeking, seeping, selling, setting, shipping, shocking, shopping, singing, sipping, sitting, slamming, slapping, sledding, sleeting, slimming, sling, slinging, slumping, sobbing, stabbing, staying, stemming, stepping, stocking, stopping, swelling, swimming, swing, swinging, tagging, tanning, tapping, telling, testing, thing, thinking, tipping, tracking, trapping, trimming, trucking, trusting, trying, tugging, turning, twirling, wagging, weeding, weeping, willing, wing, winging, winning, wishing, zing, zinging*

ADDING ON: Call out a verb such as *run*. The class repeats the word, adding and signing *ing*.

THE MATCHING GAME: Give large cards on which *ing* is written to half of your students. The other students are given cards on which one of the following consonants or blends is written: *br, d, fl, k, p, r, s, sl, spr, sw, th, w,* or *z*. Review the sign of each letter as the cards are distributed. Each child will attempt to find a partner whose "word part" will combine with his/hers to create a word.

Enrichment Activity

The sign for *ing* is a combination of the signs for *i, n,* and *g.* Allow advanced students to create their own shortcut sign for other common letter combinations such as *i, n,* and *k.*

Student Take-Home Book – *A Wedding Day*

NOTES

LESSON 32 – *x*

Previously taught letters: long *e, m, s, w,* short *u,* long *i, b, n* (and silent *e*), *z, r, p,* long *o,* long *a, h, y* (long-*i* sound), *d, g, j, f, t,* short *a, k, c, L,* short *i,* short *e, sh, er/ir/ur,* short *o, th, ing*

Lesson focus words: *fox, next*

Sign Description

Cross the index and middle finger of your left hand to roughly form an *x* shape, as illustrated.

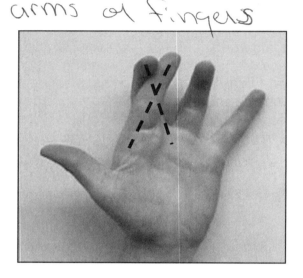

arms of fingers

Procedures

1. Demonstrate the *x* sign while making the *x* sound.

2. Review the *f,* short-*o, n,* short-*e,* and *t* signs.

3. Demonstrate blending the signs to make the words *fox* and *next.*

4. Introduce the sight words *you* and *said.*

Student Page – #32

TEXT: Next a fox came by. "You need a bath," she said. The fox kept running, and the pig kept sleeping.

ILLUSTRATION: Draw a picture of a fox talking to the pig.

Extension Activities

WORD CHALLENGE: *ax, box, fix, mix, ox, sax, six*

X RACE: Prepare flashcards for, and review, the words *box, fix, fox, next,* and *ox.* Call one student to the front of the class. When you flash one of the *x*-word cards, the class attempts to read the word before the student at the front can cross his/her fingers to make the *x* sign.

FIX IT: Call three students to the front of the room. Assign each of the three students one letter from the word *six* and line them up so the word is spelled from left to right facing the class. Instruct each of the three students, beginning with the one holding the letter *s,* to sign his/her letter and make the letter sound. The rest of the class guesses the word. Repeat with other WORD CHALLENGE words.

Enrichment Activity

FANCY EXIT: Instruct students to paint decorative EXIT signs, which will be displayed around the inside of the classroom exit door.

Student Take-Home Book – *Fox Tricks*

NOTES

LESSON 33 – long *u*

Previously taught letters: long *e, m, s, w,* short *u,* long *i, b, n* (and silent *e*), *z, r, p,* long *o,* long *a, h, y* (long-*i* sound), *d, g, j, f, t,* short *a, k, c, L,* short *i,* short *e, sh, er/ir/ur,* short *o, th, ing, x*

Lesson focus words: *cute, mule*

Sign Description

Make the short-*u* sign (see LESSON 5). Then extend your hand and forearm forward as if pointing to someone while making the long-*u* sound. Associate the sign with the sound of the word *you.* (Explain that it normally is not polite to point, but this is an exception.)

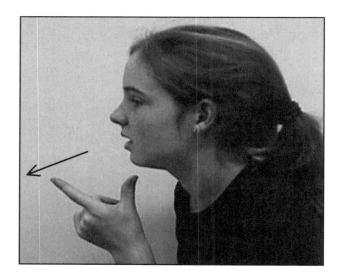

Procedures

1. Demonstrate the long-*u* sign, making the long-*u* sound as the sign is made.

2. Review the *m, L, c,* silent-*e,* and *t* signs.

3. Demonstrate blending the signs to make the words *cute* and *mule.*

4. Discuss the *ed* suffix. Explain that this suffix is signed as a chunk (short *e* and *d*). (It can be explained at a later date that the *ed* suffix sometimes makes either the *d* or *t* sound.)

Student Page – #33

TEXT: A cute mule trotted up to the pig. "Hi, pig. You are cute, but you need a bath," he said. Then the mule kept going, and the pig kept sleeping.

ILLUSTRATION: Draw a picture of a mule talking to the pig.

Extension Activities

WORD CHALLENGE: *muse, mute, tune, unicorn, uniform, unite, use*

THINGS WE USE: Discuss the sign for the word *use* (signed long *u*, *s*, silent *e*; the *s* sound should be approximated). Label a display "Things We Use." Instruct the students to clip a magazine picture of an item they sometimes use. One at a time the children go to the front of the room and sign "I use _____," signing the word *use* and filling in the blank with the name of the item in the picture.

Enrichment Activity

UNITE: Discuss and sign the word *unite,* stressing the *u* sound at the beginning. Instruct students to wander around in a cleared space in the room as music is played softly. When you say the word *unite,* they are to make the *u* sign and sound, ending it with a left-handed handshake with someone nearby. Anyone without a partner after 15 seconds is out of the game.

Student Take-Home Book – *The Mule*

NOTES

TAKE A BREATHER

Although no new sign is needed for additional ways of spelling various vowel sounds, this concept needs to be discussed. So … "take a breather" from new signs and construct a chart like the one in LESSON 13 for listing an additional way to spell the long- and short-*e* sounds.

Long *e*		Short *e*
ea		*ea*
bead	leash	bread
beak	neat	dread
beam	peas	dead
bean	plead	head
beat	please	lead
bleak	pleat	read
clean	reap	read
clear	rear	ready
cleat	sea	stead
cream	seal	tread
deal	seam	weather
dear	seat	
dream	sheath	
ear	steal	
fear	steam	
feat	streamr	
freak	tea	
gear	teal	
gleam	team	
grease	tear	
heal	tease	
heap	treat	
hear	weak	
heat	zeal	
Jean		
leaf		
leak		
lean		
leap		

LESSON 34 – *y* (long *e*)

> **Previously taught letters:** long *e, m, s, w,* short *u,* long *i, b, n* (and silent *e*), *z, r, p,* long *o,* long *a, h, y* (long-*i* sound), *d, g, j, f, t,* short *a, k, c, L,* short *i,* short *e, sh, er/ir/ur,* short *o, th, ing, x,* long *u*
>
> **Lesson focus words:** *pony, Tony, funny*

Sign Description

Make a *y* shape with the left hand at chest level. Quickly close the fingers to convert the *y* shape into an *e* shape as the *e* sound is made. Explain that *y* sometimes sounds like *e* when it comes at the end of a word.

Procedures

1. Demonstrate the *y* (long-*e*) sign, making the *y* (long-*e*) sound as the sign is made.

2. Review the *p,* long-*o, n, t, f,* and short-*u* signs.

3. Demonstrate blending the signs to make the words *pony, Tony,* and *funny.*

Student Page – #34

TEXT: A pony named Tony trotted up. "That pig smells funny," he said. Then the pony kept going, and the pig kept sleeping.

ILLUSTRATION: Draw a picture of a pony named Tony talking to the pig.

Extension Activity

WORD CHALLENGE: *batty, buddy, buggy, bumpy, bunny, clammy, crabby, creepy, crusty, curly, daddy, Danny, dirty, dolly, fatty, fishy, flabby, flirty, floppy, frilly, funny, fussy, fuzzy, grassy, greedy, gritty, grubby, grumpy, gummy, hilly, jerky, jumpy, junky, lucky, lumpy, messy, misty, mommy, muddy, perky, puppy, runny, rusty, silly, sleepy, sticky sunny, tacky, thorny, tricky*

Enrichment Activity

ADD-A-*Y:* Read a list of words to which the letter *y* can be added at the end (base words from the WORD CHALLENGE list). Students repeat the words, adding the *e* sound while making the *y* sign. For example, when you say *fun,* the students will say *funny* while making the *y* (long-*e*) sign.

Student Take-Home Book – *Dolly and Molly*

NOTES

LESSON 35 – *ow/ou*

Previously taught letters: long *e*, *m*, *s*, *w*, short *u*, long *i*, *b*, *n* (and silent *e*), *z*, *r*, *p*, long *o*, long *a*, *h*, *y* (long-*i* sound), *d*, *g*, *j*, *f*, *t*, short *a*, *k*, *c*, *L*, short *i*, short *e*, *sh*, *er/ir/ur*, short *o*, *th*, *ing*, *x*, long *u*, *y* (long-*e* sound)

Lesson focus words: *cow, frown, wow, brown, now*

Sign Description

Shake your hand, as if in pain, while making the *ow/ou* sound.

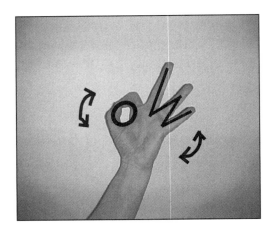

Procedures

1. Demonstrate the *ow/ou* sign, making the *ow* sound as the sign is made.

2. Review the signs for hard *c*, *fr*, *n*, *w*, and *br*.

3. Demonstrate blending the signs to make the words *cow, frown, wow, brown,* and *now*.

Student Page – #35

TEXT: A cow came by and said with a frown, "Wow. How did a pink pig get so brown?
You need a bath now." Then the cow kept going, and the pig kept sleeping.

ILLUSTRATION: Draw a picture of a cow talking to the pig.

Extension Activities

WORD CHALLENGE: *about, bound, brow, cloud, crowd, crown, down, drown, flour, flower, found, gown, growl, hound, how, howl, jowl, loud, louse, mound, mouse, mouth, noun, our, out, owl, pound, pout, plow, pow, power, proud, prowl, round, rout, shout, shower, sound, south, stout, tower, town, trout, wound*

HOW NOW, BROWN COW: List the words *now, how,* and *cow* on the board, then practice their signs with the class. Tell the students that they are to sign the words as you read them in random order. Explain that your pace will get faster and faster as you read – and they should try to keep up with you. After several tries, additional words (such as *wow* and *pow)* can be added to the list.

Enrichment Activity

A TROUT THAT SHOUTS AND POUTS: Write the following poem on a chart and read it with the class. On the second reading instruct the students to make the *ow/ou* sign when a word containing that sound is read:

What is your book about? My book is about a trout …
A trout that shouts and pouts: That's what my book is about.

Student Take-Home Book – *In a Tree*

NOTES

if its the (u) close your fingers together.

LESSON 36 – *wh*

> **Previously taught letters:** long *e, m, s, w,* short *u,* long *i, b, n* (and silent *e*), *z, r, p,* long *o,* long *a, h, y* (long-*i* sound), *d, g, j, f, t,* short *a, k, c, L,* short *i,* short *e, sh,* er/ir/ur, short *o, th, ing, x,* long *u, y* (long-*e* sound), *ow/ou*
>
> **Lesson focus words:** *white, whiskers, whispered, why, when*

Sign Description

Make a *w* shape with the three middle fingers of your left hand. Fan the *w* shape across your face as you make the *wh* sound, so that the force of air can be felt on your fingers as they cross in front of your lips.

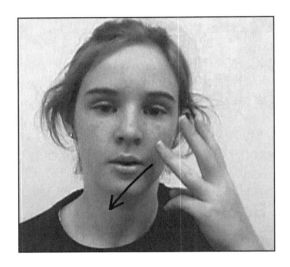

Procedures

1. Demonstrate the *wh* sign, making the *wh* sound as the sign is made.

2. Review the long-*i, sk, s, p, d, y* (long-*i* sound), short-*e, n,* short-*i, er, ed,* and *t* signs, as well as the silent-*e* concept.

3. Demonstrate blending the signs to make the words *white, whiskers, whispered, why,* and *when.*

Student Page – #36

TEXT: A white rabbit with whiskers came hopping by. "That is a messy pig," he said. "Why are you so dirty, and when did you play in the mud?" But the pig kept sleeping, so the white rabbit kept hopping.

ILLUSTRATION: Draw a picture of a white rabbit talking to the pig.

Extension Activities

WORD CHALLENGE: *whack, whale, wham, whap, wheel, whiff, while, whim, whine, whip, whir, whirl, whiz, whopper*

WHISPER: Students sit in a circle and in unison make the *wh* sign as they whisper the word *whisper*. The first student whispers his/her favorite *wh* word. Once again all students say *whisper* and make the *wh* sign. Then the second child whispers his/her favorite *wh* word, continuing until everyone has had a turn.

Enrichment Activity

WH RIDDLES: Ask *wh* riddles for students to answer, giving such clues as "This *wh* word rhymes with girl," etc. Students are expected to make the *wh* sign when guessing.

Student Take-Home Book – *Why Tom Whines*

NOTES

LESSON 37 – *y* (consonant)

> **Previously taught letters:** long *e, m, s, w,* short *u,* long *i, b, n* (and silent *e*), *z, r, p,* long *o,* long *a, h, y* (long-*i* sound), *d, g, j, f, t,* short *a, k, c, L,* short *i,* short *e, sh, er/ir/ur,* short *o, th, ing, x,* long *u, y* (long-*e* sound), *ow/ou, wh*
>
> **Lesson focus words:** *yes, yuck*

Sign Description

Draw an imaginary *y* shape on your thumb, index finger, and palm. Point with your index finger into your mouth while making the consonant-*y* sound.

Procedures

1. Demonstrate the consonant-*y* sign, making the consonant-*y* sound as the sign is made.

2. Review the short-*u, ck,* short-*e,* and *s* signs.

3. Demonstrate blending the signs to make the words *yes* and *yuck.*

Student Page – #37

TEXT: A duck and her duckling came by. "Yuck," said the duck. Her duckling said, "Yes, that is a yucky pig." Then the ducks kept going, and the pig kept sleeping.

ILLUSTRATION: Draw a picture of a duck and her duckling talking to the pig.

Extension Activities

WORD CHALLENGE: *yak, yam, yap, yard, yell, yelling, yelp, yesterday, yet, yip, yippee, yoke, yolk, yucky, yum, yummy*

YES OR *NO?* Practice signing and reading the word *yes*. Ask a series of *yes/no* questions to which the children are expected to respond by signing *yes* or *no*.

Enrichment Activity

YUMMY OR YUCKY? Each child will label half a sheet of paper *Yummy* and the other half *Yucky*, then glue pictures of foods on the side that best describes their fondness (or lack of it) for the food pictured.

Student Take-Home Book – *Yummy or Yucky?*

NOTES

LESSON 38 – *ch*

Previously taught letters: long *e*, *m*, *s*, *w*, short *u*, long *i*, *b*, *n* (and silent *e*), *z*, *r*, *p*, long *o*, long *a*, *h*, *y* (long-*i* sound), *d*, *g*, *j*, *f*, *t*, short *a*, *k*, *c*, *L*, short *i*, short *e*, *sh*, *er/ir/ur*, short *o*, *th*, *ing*, *x*, long *u*, *y* (long-*e* sound), *ow/ou*, *wh*, *y* (consonant)

Lesson focus words: *chirp, such, chum*

Sign Description

Make the *c* sign and move your hand to resemble a train chugging along while making the *ch* sound.

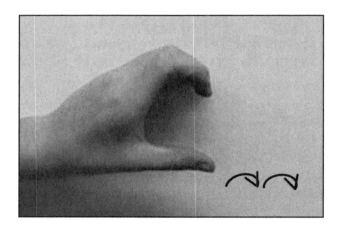

Procedures

1. Demonstrate the *ch* sign while making the *ch* sound.

2. Review the *ir, p, s,* short-*u,* and *m* signs.

3. Blend the signs to make the words *chirp, such,* and *chum.*

Student Page – #38

<u>Note</u>: *Although the* ed *suffix is sometimes pronounced* t, *it should be signed with the* e-d *signs, and the sound should be approximated.*

TEXT: A bird hopped by. "Chirp, chirp. Such a messy chum," the bird sang. But the pig kept sleeping, so the bird kept hopping.

ILLUSTRATION: Draw a picture of a bird talking to the pig.

Extension Activities

WORD CHALLENGE: *batch, beach, birch, breech, bunch, Chad, chap, chat, cheap, cheat, check, cheep, cheer, cheese, chill, chime, chin, chip, choke, chop, chopper, chore, chow, chubby, chum, chunk, chunky, church, ditch, kitchen, latch, leach, match, much, patch, pitch, pouch, rich, scratch, snatch*

CH-CH TRAIN: Label a display "*Ch-Ch* Train." Clip *ch* words from the newspaper. Glue words that begin with *ch* onto the engine, words with *ch* in the middle onto the center car, and words that end with *ch* onto the caboose.

TRAIN WHISTLE: When a student correctly names a word that begins with *ch*, blow a train whistle!

Enrichment Activity

SANDWICH WORDS: Explain that *church* is a sandwich word: It begins and ends with the same letter(s). Write *ch* on a sheet of paper trimmed to resemble a slice of bread, then repeat to form the second slice of bread for a sandwich. Write the letters *ur* on paper cut to resemble bologna or another sandwich filler and display the three word parts on a board labeled "Sandwich Words." Brainstorm additional sandwich words (*Dad, did, dread, maim, Mom, shush, tot,* etc.).

Student Take-Home Book – *Chubby Chad*

NOTES

LESSON 39 – *ar*

Previously taught letters: long *e*, *m*, *s*, *w*, short *u*, long *i*, *b*, *n* (and silent *e*), *z*, *r*, *p*, long *o*, long *a*, *h*, *y* (long-*i* sound), *d*, *g*, *j*, *f*, *t*, short *a*, *k*, *c*, *L*, short *i*, short *e*, *sh*, *er/ir/ur*, short *o*, *th*, *ing*, *x*, long *u*, *y* (long-*e* sound), *ow/ou*, *wh*, *y* (consonant), *ch*

Lesson focus words: *dark*, *far*

Sign Description

Move your hand forward, as a wildcat might do with its paw, when roaring *ar.*

Procedures

1. Demonstrate the *ar* sign, making the *ar* sound as the sign is made.

2. Review the *d*, *k*, and *f* signs.

3. Demonstrate blending the signs to make the words *dark* and *far.*

4. Introduce the sight word *was.*

Student Page – #39

TEXT: It got dark. The pig was still far from home.

ILLUSTRATION: Draw a picture of the pig at nighttime.

Extension Activities

WORD CHALLENGE: *alarm, are, arm, bar, barb, bark, barn, Bart, car, card, cart, charm, chart, Clark, dart, farm, farmer, garb, hard, hark, harm, harp, jar, lard, lark, mark, shark, star, start, tar, tarp, tart, yarn*

ARE YOU? Practice reading and signing the word *are* (*ar*, silent *e*). Ask a series of questions to which the children would respond positively. The students will respond by making the *ar* sign and saying, "We are." Sample questions: "Are you ready for lunch? Are you looking forward to playing in the gym? Are you excited about going on the field trip?"

Enrichment Activities

AR CARS: Write *ar* words on racecars. Try to accumulate enough cars to create a line long enough to reach a designated finish line.

AR ART: Read and sign the word *art* with the class. Instruct students to write the word *art* in a decorative fashion. Display the word designs near the art center.

AR POEM/SONG (sing to the tune of "Twinkle, Twinkle, Little Star"):

> Twinkle, twinkle, little star,
> How I wonder what you are;
> Up above the world so far,
> Like a headlight on my car;
> Twinkle, twinkle, little star,
> How I wonder what you are.

DARTBOARD *AR* WORDS: Introduce the word *dart*. Using child-safe darts, create a dartboard that lists *ar* words in each section. The child must pronounce the word in the section that his/her dart hits.

Student Take-Home Book – *Shark at Sea*

NOTES

LESSON 40 – long *oo* (spelled *oo* and *ew*)

> **Previously taught letters:** long *e, m, s, w,* short *u,* long *i, b, n* (and silent *e*), *z, r, p,* long *o,* long *a, h, y* (long-*i* sound), *d, g, j, f, t,* short *a, k, c, L,* short *i,* short *e, sh, er/ir/ur,* short *o, th, ing, x,* long *u, y* (long-*e* sound), *ow/ou, wh, y* (consonant), *ch, ar*
>
> **Lesson focus words:** goose, too, new, moon, soon

Sign Description

Form the *o* shape at chest level, same as for the long-*o* sound. Gently shake your hand while making the long-*oo* sound; explain that your hand is shaking because of the scary *oo* sound. Alternative sign: Hold your nose as if in response to a foul odor while saying "*oo.*"

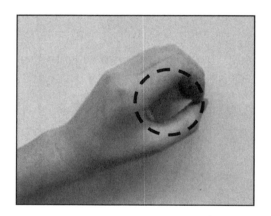 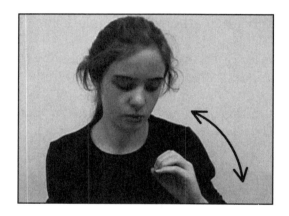

Procedures

1. Demonstrate the long-*oo* sign, making the long-*oo* sound while making the sign.

2. Review the *t* sign.

3. Demonstrate blending the *t* and *oo* signs to make the word *too.*

4. Follow a similar procedure to introduce the words *goose, flew, too, new, moon,* and *soon.*

Student Page – #40

TEXT: A goose flew by. "You are too dirty," said the goose. "The new moon will be out soon." Then the goose kept flying, and the pig kept sleeping.

ILLUSTRATION: Draw a picture of a goose talking to the pig.

Extension Activities

WORD CHALLENGE: *baboon, bloom, boo, boom, boot, brood, broom, caboose, chew, cool, coon, coop, crew, dew, doom, drew, food, goofy, grew, groom, hoop, Jew, loon, loose, moo, mood, noon, noose, pooch, Pooh, pool, scoot, shoot, smooth, stew, stoop, tool, toot, troop, whoop, zoo, zoom*

TOO MUCH, GOOFY: Discuss the meaning of the word *too.* Read and sign the words *toot* and *Goofy.* Allow a puppet named Goofy to guess numbers, such as the number of students in the class and the number of teachers, desks, coats, lunchboxes, etc., in the classroom. When Goofy's guess is too high, the children sign the word *too* and say, "Too much, Goofy."

Enrichment Activities

RACCOON MASKS: Make masks out of black circles (similar to a pair of glasses with very thick rims) to resemble a raccoon mask. Instruct students to sign and read *oo* words while wearing the masks.

TOOT – OR TOOT? Point out that the word *toot* is spelled the same forward and backward. Brainstorm other palindromes.

BABOONS: Discuss baboons and read the word.

Student Take-Home Book – *Moose and Goose*

NOTES

LESSON 41 – v

Previously taught letters: long *e*, *m*, *s*, *w*, short *u*, long *i*, *b*, *n* (and silent *e*), *z*, *r*, *p*, long *o*, long *a*, *h*, *y* (long-*i* sound), *d*, *g*, *j*, *f*, *t*, short *a*, *k*, *c*, *L*, short *i*, short *e*, *sh*, *er/ir/ur*, short *o*, *th*, *ing*, *x*, long *u*, *y* (long-*e* sound), *ow/ou*, *wh*, *y* (consonant), *ch*, *ar*, long *oo* (spelled *oo* and *ew*)

Lesson focus words: *five, dive*

Sign Description

Make a *v* shape with the index and middle finger of your left hand, as illustrated. Place the *v* shape on your chest, as if forming the neckline of a vest.

Procedures

1. Demonstrate the *v* sign while making the *v* sound.

2. Review the *f*, *d*, silent-*e*, and long-*i* signs.

3. Blend the signs to make the words *five* and *dive*.

Student Page – #41

TEXT: Five deer ran by. "You are so dirty," one deer said. "You should dive into the lake." The five deer kept running, while the pig kept sleeping.

ILLUSTRATION: Draw a picture of five deer talking to the pig.

Extension Activities

WORD CHALLENGE: *arrive, carve, crave, drive, grove, rave, rove, shave, starve, stove, stoves, swerve, vane, vast, veal, vest, vet, Vicky, vile, vim, vine, vote, votes, wives*

VICTORY: Explain how the *v* sign has been used for many years as a symbol of victory. Write a word on the board for a child to sign and read. If the child reads the word correctly, the rest of the students make a *v* sign and say, "Victory!"

Enrichment Activities

V VESTS: Make each child a vest from a brown paper grocery bag by cutting up the front, then cutting holes for the head and each arm. Each child may cover the vest with words that begin with the letter *v* or with pictures of objects, the names of which begin with *v*.

V VALENTINES: Demonstrate how the letter *v* can be connected at the top to become a heart-shaped valentine. Fill a large valentine shape with *v* words clipped from newspapers or magazines.

Student Take-Home Book – *Can a Rooster?*

NOTES

LESSON 42 – short *oo*

> **Previously taught letters:** long *e, m, s, w,* short *u,* long *i, b, n* (and silent *e*), *z, r, p,* long *o,* long *a, h, y* (long-*i* sound), *d, g, j, f, t,* short *a, k, c, L,* short *i,* short *e, sh, er/ir/ur,* short *o, th, ing, x,* long *u, y* (long-*e* sound), *ow/ou, wh, y* (consonant), *ch, ar,* long *oo* (spelled *oo* and *ew*), *v*
>
> **Lesson focus words:** *look, took, shook, brook*

Sign Description

Form the *o* shape at ear level. Gently shake your hand while making the short-*o* sound.

Procedures

1. Demonstrate the short-*oo* sign, making the short-*oo* sound as the sign is made.

2. Review the *L, t, sh, br,* and *k* signs.

3. Demonstrate blending the signs to make the words *look, took, shook,* and *brook.*

Student Page – #42

TEXT: An owl took a look at the pig. She shook her wings. "Just look," she said. "Go jump into the brook." The owl did not stop. She just kept flying, and the pig kept sleeping.

ILLUSTRATION: Draw a picture of an owl flying over the pig.

Extension Activity

WORD CHALLENGE: *book, cook, crook, good, hood, hoof, hook, nook, stood, wood, woof, wool*

OO RIDDLES: List the following letters on the board: *b, c, L, n, sh,* and *t.* Ask the students riddles that begin with one of the letters listed and end with *ook.* Sample riddle: This word describes something that has pages and words in it.

Enrichment Activity

HOW TO COOK A ROOK: Discuss the words *rook, nook,* and *brook,* then read the following poem:

> "Just look at this book," said the rook.
> The rook shook as we took a look.
> "I cooked from this book in my nook by the brook ...
> Till I read, 'How to cook a rook.'"

Student Take-Home Book – *Goody, Goody, Goody*

NOTES

LESSON 43 – *aw* (spelled *aw, au, a[l]*, and *a[ll]*)

> **Previously taught letters:** long *e, m, s, w,* short *u,* long *i, b, n* (and silent *e*), *z, r, p,* long *o,* long *a, h, y* (long-*i* sound), *d, g, j, f, t,* short *a, k, c, L,* short *i,* short *e, sh, er/ir/ur,* short *o, th, ing, x,* long *u, y* (long-*e* sound), *ow/ou, wh, y* (consonant), *ch, ar,* long *oo* (spelled *oo* and *ew*), *v,* short *oo*
>
> **Lesson focus words:** *all, crawling, saw, walk*

Sign Description

Hold your left hand at shoulder level with your palm facing outward. Allow your hand to drop forward (as if in disbelief) while making the *aw* sound.

Procedures

1. Demonstrate the *aw* sign, making the *aw* sound as the sign is made.

2. Explain that *a* followed by *L* or *ll* also spells the *aw* sound, as in the word *tall*. The word tall is signed with the *t, aw*, and *L* signs.

3. Explain that *au* also spells the *aw* sound.

4. Review the *s, L, cr, ing, w, p,* and *k* signs.

5. Demonstrate blending the signs to make the words *all, crawling, saw, Paul,* and *walk*. Introduce the sight words *friend* and *have*.

Student Page – #43

TEXT: Last of all a skunk named Paul crawled up to the pig. The pig woke up. She saw the skunk. "Hello," said the pig. The skunk was glad to have a friend. "You smell nice," said the skunk. "So do you," said the pig. The skunk said, " I will walk all the way home with you."

ILLUSTRATION: Draw a picture of a skunk talking to the pig.

Extension Activities

WORD CHALLENGE: *balk, call, caw, chalk, claw, dawn, draw, drawl, drawn, fall, flaw, gall, haul, hawk, jaw, law, lawn, lawyer, mall, Paul, paw, pawn, raw, shawl, slaw, stalk, stall, talk, tall, wall, Wal-Mart*

AWE-SOME: Discuss the word *awe*. Sign the word with the class. Call on students one at a time to tell something that they think is *awesome*. After each response, the class makes the *aw* sign and says, "Awesome!"

Enrichment Activity

I SAW E-SAW: Read the "I Saw E-Saw" poem with the class. (Explain that E-Saw is a name that can be spelled several different ways. It is spelled differently – Esau – in the Bible.)

> I saw E-Saw drawing on a seesaw.
> I saw E-Saw; he saw me.

Student Take-Home Book – *Can I?*

NOTES

LESSON 44 – *tion*

> **Previously taught letters:** long *e, m, s, w,* short *u,* long *i, b, n* (and silent *e*), *z, r, p,* long *o,* long *a, h, y* (long-*i* sound), *d, g, j, f, t,* short *a, k, c, L,* short *i,* short *e, sh, er/ir/ur,* short *o, th, ing, x,* long *u, y* (long-*e* sound), *ow/ou, wh, y* (consonant), *ch, ar,* long *oo* (spelled *oo* and *ew*), *v,* short *oo, aw* (spelled *aw, au, a[l],* and *a[ll]*)
>
> **Lesson focus words:** *notion, motion, action, vacation, nation*

Sign Description

Because the *tion* word chunk starts with the letter *t,* we begin as if to make the *t* sign close to the face. Then, as if suddenly realizing we are about to make a mistake, we quickly move into the *sh* sign and say "shun."

Procedures

1. Demonstrate the *tion* sign.

2. Review the *m, n,* short-*a,* hard-*c,* long-*o, v,* and long-*a* signs.

3. Demonstrate blending the signs to form the words *notion, motion, action, vacation,* and *nation.*

4. Introduce *they* and *somewhere* as sight words.

© Bethanie H. Tucker • **aha!** Process, Inc. • (800) 424-9484

Student Page – #44

TEXT: When the pig takes a notion to play a game, she will motion for the skunk. These friends play action games. They may even take a vacation somewhere in the nation!

ILLUSTRATION: Draw a picture of the skunk and the pig playing together.

Extension Activities

WORD CHALLENGE: *aviation, creation, inflation, lotion, oration, ovation, perfection, portion, potion, quotation, vocation*

SLOW MOTION: Practice signing the word *motion.* Discuss slow motion. With the class, sign the *m-o* in slow motion, then quickly make the • *tion* sign.

Enrichment Activity

GROWN-UP WORDS: Explain to your students that learning the *tion* sign will help them be able to read grown-up words. Write the following words on the board one at a time, allowing a student to circle the *tion* in each word as the class makes the *tion* sign. Pronounce each word for the class and briefly discuss the meaning of such words as *aggravation, elevation, gravitation, location, locomotion, motivation* and *rotation.*

Student Take-Home Book – *Men in Motion*

NOTES

APPENDIX

Soft *g*

The soft-*g* sound can be signed by forming the shape of the *g* sign with the left hand, then drawing the *j* shape in the air (rather than holding the hand at the throat) while making the soft-*g* (*j*) sound.

Soft *c*

A teacher at Sacred Heart School, Danville, Virginia, suggested the following sign for the soft-*c* sound: Review the hard-*c* cutting motion. Explain that scissors sometimes cut paper (make the cutting motion with the left hand). Sometimes, however, scissors tear paper. (Thrust your left hand forward as if using your <u>scissors</u> fingers to tear paper.)

Q/qu

No sign was developed for the letter *Q,* but a group of second-graders at Happy Home Primary School, Rockingham County, North Carolina, developed the following sign: Explain that the letter *q* is almost always followed by a *u.* The word *queen* starts with *qu.* To make a *qu* sign, draw a circle around your face, as if you are the queen, while making the *qu* (*kw*) sound. When your left hand reaches the top of your head, form a *u* shape and put the *u* on top of your head for a crown.

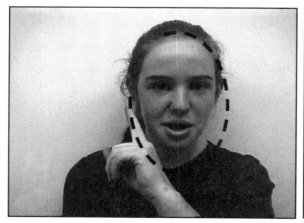 

MY BOOK

ILLUSTRATED BY

_____

_____

Name: _____   LESSON 1: long *e*

Directions: Draw a picture of yourself and something that frightens you
and makes you say "eeeee."

Name: _____   LESSON 2: *m*

Directions: Draw a picture of yourself.

Me

Directions: Draw a picture of yourself doing something exciting.

See me.

Name: _____   LESSON 4: *w*

Directions: Draw a picture of yourself doing something exciting while
two of your friends are watching.

We see.

Name: _____

Directions: Draw a picture of yourself having fun with two friends.

See us.

Name: _____   LESSON 6: long *i*

Directions: Draw a picture of yourself looking at something behind a rock.
             Your friends are waiting for you to tell them what you see.

I see ...

Name: _____   LESSON 7: *b*

Directions: Draw a picture of bees flying over your head.

bees!

Name: _____   LESSON 8: *n* (and silent *e*)

Directions: Draw a picture of nine bees.

Nine bees ...

Name: _____   LESSON 9: *z*

Directions: Draw a picture of some bees, then write the word "buzz" beside each one.

buzz.

Name: _____

Directions: Draw a picture of you and your friends running away from
the bees.

Run, run!

Name: _____   LESSON 11: p

Directions: Draw a picture of you and your friends running up a hill.

Run up!

Name: _____

Directions: Draw a picture of you and your friends at the top of the hill. You are happy because there are no bees there.

I see no bees.

Name: _____

Directions: Draw a picture of a puppy.

I see a pup.

Tucker Signing Strategies for Reading © Bethanie H. Tucker • **aha!** Process, Inc. • (800) 424-9484

Name: _____   LESSON 14: *h*

Directions: Draw a picture of yourself petting the pup.

Hi, pup.

Name: _____   LESSON 15: *y* (long-*i* sound)

Directions: Draw a picture of you and your horse.

I see my horse.

     Tucker Signing Strategies for Reading © Bethanie H. Tucker • **aha!** Process, Inc. • (800) 424-9484

Name: _____   LESSON 16: *d*

Directions: Draw a picture of you and your friends riding your horse.

Ride my horse.

Name: _____

Directions: Draw a picture of your horse running.

See us go.

Tucker Signing Strategies for Reading © Bethanie H. Tucker • **aha!** Process, Inc. • (800) 424-9484

Name: _____ LESSON 18: *j*

Directions: Draw a picture of your horse jumping over something.

See us jump.

Name: _____

Directions: Draw a picture of you and your friends smiling as you ride your
           horse.

Fun, fun, fun.

Name: _____   LESSON 20: *t*

Directions: Draw a picture of you and your friends sitting on the ground
            beside your horse.

Time for ...

Name: _____   LESSON 21: short *a*

Directions: Draw a picture of you and your friends sleeping.

a nap.

Tucker Signing Strategies for Reading © Bethanie H. Tucker • **aha!** Process, Inc. • (800) 424-9484

Name: _____

Directions: Draw a picture of you and your friends awake.

Wake up! Wake up!
Time to go home.

Name: _____   LESSON 23: *c*

Directions: Draw a picture of your horse running fast.

My horse can run fast.

Name: _____ LESSON 24: *L*

Directions: Draw a picture of you and your friends at your house.

Home at last.

Name: _____   LESSON 25: short *i*

Directions: Draw a picture of a pig.

I see a pig. It is a pink pig, and it is big.

Tucker Signing Strategies for Reading © Bethanie H. Tucker • **aha!** Process, Inc. • (800) 424-9484

Directions: Draw a picture of your pet pig playing in the mud.

It is my pet pig. I let
my pet play in wet
mud.

Name: _____   LESSON 27: *sh*

Directions: Draw a picture of your pet pig covered with mud.

She is a mess.

Directions: Draw a picture of your pet pig running away.

My pig is a girl. Her name is Furl. One day Furl ran away.

Name: _____

Directions: Draw a picture of your pet pig asleep.

It was a summer day.
My pig got hot. She
went to sleep.

Name: _____   LESSON 30: *th*

Directions: Draw a picture of a thin sheep looking at the sleeping pig.

A thin sheep with thick hair came by. The thin sheep sat by the pig.

Name: _____

Directions: Draw a picture of the sheep walking away.

But the pig kept sleeping, so the sheep got up and kept going.

Name: _____

Directions: Draw a picture of a fox talking to the pig.

Next a fox came by. "You need a bath," she said. The fox kept running, and the pig kept sleeping.

Name: _____

Directions: Draw a picture of a mule talking to the pig.

A cute mule trotted up to the pig. "Hi, pig. You are cute, but you need a bath," he said. Then the mule kept going, and the pig kept sleeping.

Name: _____   LESSON 34: *y* (long-*e* sound)

Directions: Draw a picture of a pony named Tony talking to the pig.

A pony named Tony trotted up. "That pig smells funny," he said. Then the pony kept going, and the pig kept sleeping.

Directions: Draw a picture of a cow talking to the pig.

A cow came by and said with a frown, "Wow. How did a pink pig get so brown? You need a bath now." Then the cow kept going, and the pig kept sleeping.

Directions: Draw a picture of a white rabbit talking to the pig.

A white rabbit with whiskers came hopping by. "That is a messy pig," he said. "Why are you so dirty, and when did you play in the mud?" But the pig kept sleeping, so the white rabbit kept hopping.

Directions: Draw a picture of a duck and her duckling talking to the pig.

A duck and her duckling came by. "Yuck," said the duck. Her duckling said, "Yes, that is a yucky pig." Then the ducks kept going, and the pig kept sleeping.

Directions: Draw a picture of a bird talking to the pig.

A bird hopped by. "Chirp, chirp. Such a messy chum," the bird sang. But the pig kept sleeping, so the bird kept hopping.

Name: _____

Directions: Draw a picture of the pig at nighttime.

It got dark. The pig was still far from
home.

Name: _____   LESSON 40: long *oo* (spelled *oo*
                                                      and *ew*)

Directions: Draw a picture of a goose talking to the pig.

A goose flew by. "You are too dirty,"
said the goose. "The new moon will be
out soon." Then the goose kept flying,
and the pig kept sleeping.

Directions: Draw a picture of five deer talking to the pig.

Five deer ran by. "You are so dirty," one deer said. "You should dive into the lake." The five deer kept running, while the pig kept sleeping.

Name: _____   LESSON 42: short *oo*

Directions: Draw a picture of an owl flying over the pig.

An owl took a look at the pig. She shook her wings. "Just look," she said. "Go jump into the brook." The owl did not stop. She just kept flying, and the pig kept sleeping.

Name: _____

Directions: Draw a picture of a skunk talking to the pig.

Last of all a skunk named Paul crawled up to the pig. The pig woke up. She saw the skunk. "Hello," said the pig. The skunk was glad to have a friend. "You smell nice," said the skunk. "So do you," said the pig. The skunk said, "I will walk all the way home with you."

Name: _____

Directions: Draw a picture of the skunk and the pig playing together.

When the pig takes a notion to play a game, she will motion for the skunk. These friends play action games. They may even take a vacation somewhere in the nation!

INDEX OF SIGNS

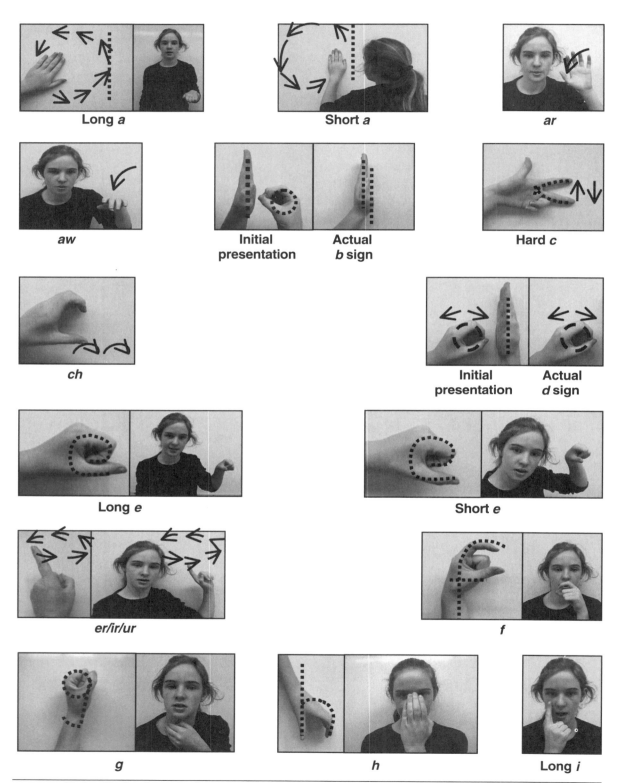

Long *a*

Short *a*

ar

aw

Initial
presentation

Actual
b sign

Hard *c*

ch

Initial
presentation

Actual
d sign

Long *e*

Short *e*

er/ir/ur

f

g

h

Long *i*

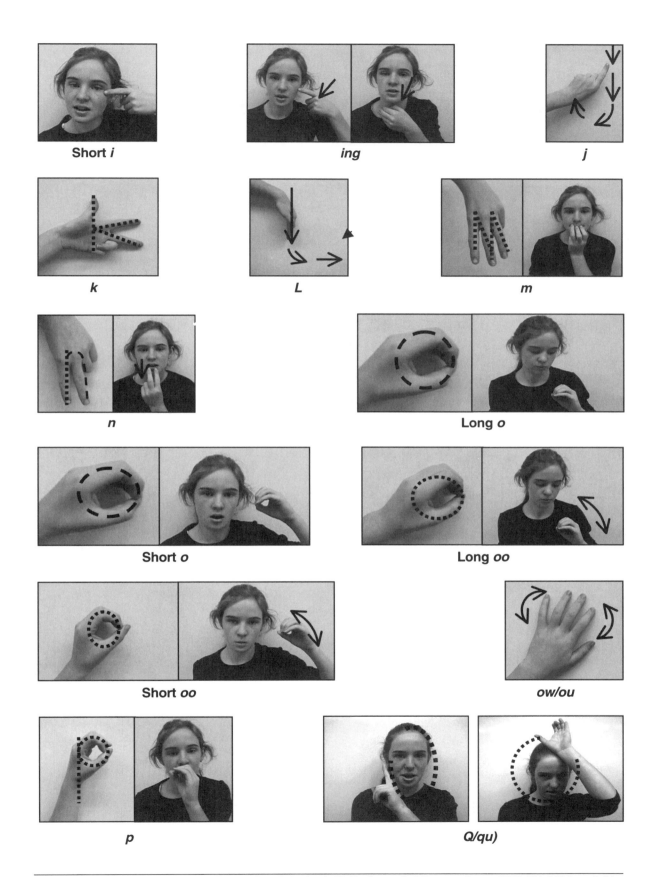

Short *i*

ing

j

k

L

m

n

Long *o*

Short *o*

Long *oo*

Short *oo*

ow/ou

p

Q/qu)

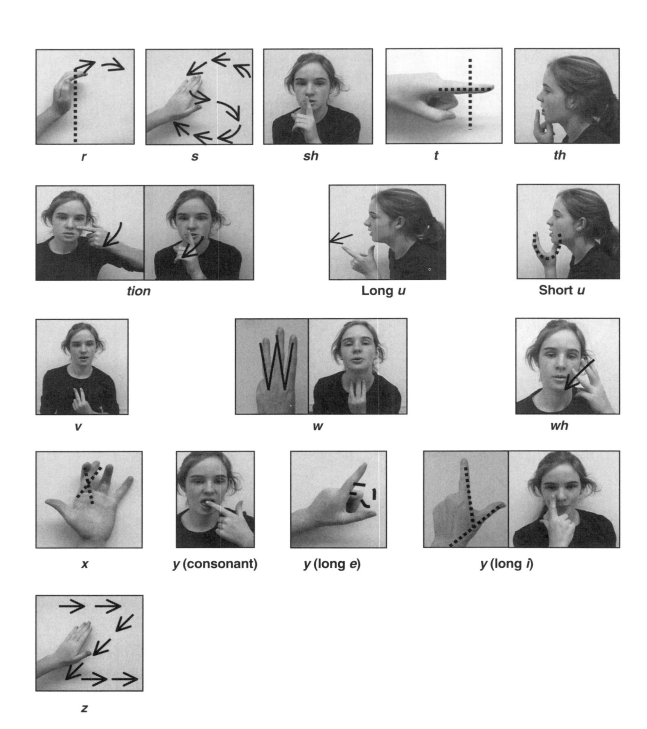

r

s

sh

t

th

tion

Long *u*

Short *u*

v

w

wh

x

y (consonant)

y (long *e*)

y (long *i*)

z

www.ahaprocess.com
PO Box 727, Highlands, TX 77562-0727
(800) 424-9484; fax: (281) 426-8705
store@ahaprocess.com

ORDER FORM

UPS SHIP TO ADDRESS: (no post office boxes, please)

NAME: _____ E-mail _____

ORGANIZATION: _____

ADDRESS: _____

CITY/STATE/ZIP: _____

TELEPHONE: _____ FAX: _____

QTY	TITLE	1-4 Copies	5+ Copies	Total
	A Framework for Understanding Poverty	22.00	15.00	
	Understanding Learning	10.00	7.00	
	A Framework for Understanding Poverty Workbook	7.00	7.00	
	Learning Structures Workbook	7.00	7.00	
	A Framework for Understanding Poverty Audio Workshop Kit (includes Day 1 & 2 audiotapes – 10 – and 4 books listed above) **S/H: $10.50**	225.00	225.00	
	Un Marco Para Entender La Pobreza	22.00	15.00	
	Putting the Pieces Together (replaces Application of Learning Structures)	10.00	10.00	
	Daily Math Practice for Virginia SOLs – Grade 4	22.00	15.00	
	Mr. Base Ten Invents Mathematics	22.00	15.00	
	Think Rather of Zebra	18.00	15.00	
	Berrytales – Plays in One Act	25.00	20.00	
	What Every Church Member Should Know About Poverty	22.00	15.00	
	A Picture Is Worth a Thousand Words	18.00	15.00	
	Parenting Someone Else's Child: The Foster Parents How-To Manual	22.00	15.00	
	Bridges Out of Poverty: Strategies for Professionals & Communities	22.00	15.00	
	Getting Ahead in a Just Gettin'-By World & Facilitator Notes (set)	25.00	25.00	
	Getting Ahead in a Just Gettin'-By World (after purchasing a set)	15.00	15.00	
	Getting Ahead in a Just Gettin'-By World Facilitator Notes (after set)	10.00	10.00	
	Removing the Mask: Giftedness in Poverty	25.00	20.00	
	Living on a Tightrope: a Survival Handbook for Principals	22.00	15.00	
	Hidden Rules of Class at Work	22.00	15.00	
	Hear Our Cry: Boys in Crisis	22.00	15.00	
	Tucker Signing Strategies Video & Manual **S/H: $8.50**	195.00	195.00	
	Tucker Signs Reference Cards on CD	25.00	25.00	
	Take-Home Books for Tucker Signing Strategies for Reading	22.00	15.00	
	Preventing School Violence – 5 videos & manual **S/H: $15.00**	995.00	995.00	
	Preventing School Violence CD – PowerPoint presentation	25.00	25.00	
	Preventing School Violence Training Manual	15.00	15.00	
	Audiotapes, What Every Church Member Should Know About Poverty	25.00	25.00	
	Meeting Standards & Raising Test Scores When You Don't Have Much Time or Money (4 videos/training manual **S/H: $15.00**	995.00	995.00	
	Meeting Standards & Raising Test Scores Training Manual	18.00	18.00	
	Meeting Standards & Raising Test Scores Resource Manual	18.00	18.00	
	Meeting Standards & Raising Test Scores CD – PowerPoint presentation	50.00	50.00	
	Rita's Stories (2 videos) **S/H: $8.50**	150.00	150.00	
	Ruby Payne Video Sampler	10.00	10.00	
	aha! 12 oz. mugs (white with red logo and website)	8.00	2 @ 15.00	
	Rubygems! 16-month calendar – Ideas for working with parents **$2 S/H**	5.00	5.00	
For Certified Trainers Only – Please note date/city of training:				
	A Framework for Understanding Poverty Video Sets (12 videos) (Day 1 & Day 2 of Framework seminar) Circle one: VHS or DVD **S/H: $25.00**	1995.00	1995.00	
	A Framework for Understanding Poverty CD – PowerPoint presentation	50.00	50.00	
	A Framework for Understanding Poverty CD – Enhanced PowerPoint pres.	100.00	100.00	
	Bridges Out of Poverty CD – PowerPoint presentation	50.00	50.00	

Total Quantity		Subtotal	
S/H: 1-4 books – $4.50 plus $2.00 each additional book up to 4 books, [1 calendar $2]		S/H	
5+ books – 8% of total, *(special S/H for videos). E-mail for international rates.*		Tax	
TAX: 8.25% Texas residents only		**Total**	

Please follow these terms when ordering. Prices subject to change.

AmEx   MC   Visa   Discover

CREDIT CARD # _____ EXP. DATE_____ Signature_____

Please see website for all current offerings

More eye-openers at ...

www.ahaprocess.com

- **To book training** or get more information on this subject:
  Contact our office at (800) 424-9484 for workshops on
  Tucker Signing Strategies for Reading by Dr. Bethanie Tucker!

- **NEW! Look for Dr. Tucker's next book, soon to be released:**

  The Journey of Al & Gebra into the Land of Algebra

- **Visit our on-line store for other related titles**

  Mr. Base Ten Invents Mathematics also by Dr. Tucker

  Tucker Take-Home Books by Melinda Ausband

  (accompanying student materials for Tucker Signing Strategies)

- **Join our aha! News List!**

  Receive the latest income and poverty statistics *free* when you join!

  Also receive a free downloadable copy of *Understanding Learning!*

  Then receive periodic news and updates, recent articles written by Dr. Ruby
  Payne, and much more!

- **Register for Dr. Ruby Payne's U. S. National Tour on *A Framework for Understanding Poverty***

- **Learn about our Trainer Certification Programs**